BUILDING
PEOPLE
through a
caring
sharing
fellowship

BUILDING PEOPLE through a caring sharing fellowship

Donald L. Bubna
with
Sarah Ricketts

LIVING STUDIES
Tyndale House Publishers, Inc.
Wheaton, Illinois

Every incident in this book is true,
and the persons referred to
have given the authors permission to tell their stories.
In a few cases, names have been changed
to protect the privacy of the individual.

Sixth printing, Living Studies edition, January 1983
Library of Congress Catalog Card Number 81-86357
ISBN 0-8423-0187-9, Living Studies edition
Copyright © 1978 by Tyndale House Publishers, Inc.,
Wheaton, Illinois
All rights reserved
Printed in the United States of America

To the believers
in Salem Alliance Church
and
Pacific Beach Bible Church
who have let me grow with them

CONTENTS

1
Love Me
As I Am

"I want to withdraw my membership from the church!" The slender woman spoke calmly into the microphone, and from the platform behind her I could see the shocked response of the people in the packed pews. Her parents' faces reflected quiet suffering as Janet's words rang through the sound system:

"I have been living a lie, and I can't continue to hide it." Only a slight tremor in her voice betrayed emotion. "Please understand that I appreciate your friendship, and I want to continue as a visitor here. But I have discovered that I don't believe in Christianity as a valid philosophy of life. Therefore, I can't remain a member of this church."

Various people reflected their surprise, disbelief, and hurt, yet another response was becoming even more evident; a wave of compassion toward the lonely figure behind the microphone. Did Janet sense it too? I hoped so, and even as I thought it, I realized that what had happened was inevitable.

I had learned some things about Janet Landis over the last four years when she had made infrequent visits to my study to unburden her increasing pain and share her often unorthodox views. Janet had grown up in the church. Her father was an elder in the congregation when I first arrived as pastor ten years before. A determined and devout man of German-Russian descent, he had been pleased when Janet, the seventh of nine children, had gone to a Bible college. There she met and married her husband, Bob. When I came to Salem, Bob was still in college, working toward his Master's degree in education, while Janet was busy with three small children. After the birth of their fourth child, she too returned to college. I saw them only occasionally in church, until Janet began coming to my office for counseling.

Her immediate purpose was to share some personal difficulties, but I soon discovered that these only masked a deeper problem often experienced by young people who grow up in the church. Janet had sincere doubt that Christianity is anything other than a standard of behavior that makes us acceptable in the eyes of family and church. Janet had been a "good girl" all her life. A straight "A" student in Bible college, she was active in the missions program, was president of the honor society, and taught Sunday school in a black inner-city church. Yet since her early teen years she had lived with questions and doubts carefully hidden behind the "game of religion" she played so well.

Only after two years in graduate school, where atheistic and agnostic professors encouraged her doubts, did she feel free to tell me her honest opinion of Christianity.

"I have to answer for myself the questions of what is real, what is good and evil, and whether man is really free . . ." she told me. Her voice was urgent. "Christianity is too narrow. I must find a philosophy of life by which I can live honestly with my imperfections and strive to be a better person on my own terms."

I felt the challenge in her dark eyes and was conscious of my own inadequacy. There was nothing I could tell her about the great truths of Christianity that she had not read or heard before. Instead I thanked her for her honesty and invited her to come by my office as often as she liked. "I will be interested to hear where you are in your struggle toward a reality in your life," I said.

Janet looked as though she expected me to say something else, but after a brief silence she nodded with a quick smile. "Thanks, Pastor, for not telling me the obvious things."

Over the next two years she came often. Each time she voiced criticism of the church as a group of narrow-minded judges, and said she was continuing her search for a valid set of goals for her own life. She seemed progressively more depressed and frustrated. She told me she had chosen what she called an existentialist philosophy, attempting to decide her own standards of right and wrong, and it disturbed her that this did not result in the sense of peace and freedom she had hoped to find.

After two years, Janet received her Master's degree in education and moved with her husband and children to Alaska, where Bob became chairman of the English Department at Ketchikan High School. I only saw Janet when she returned occasionally to Salem for a visit, and I began to sense that she was moving dangerously close to despair.

"I have made some free choices," she told me, "but I can't rid myself of the idea that some of the things I've done are morally wrong." There were dark circles under her eyes, and new lines of pain etched around her sensitive mouth. She played nervously with the frayed seam of her jeans pocket. "It doesn't make sense to feel guilt when I don't believe there are any real objective standards of right and wrong . . . yet I am not finding freedom from guilt."

"I think I understand something of what you feel," I said slowly. "I can say that because guilt is a human condition, and I am very human. Men have tried to escape guilt simply by saying there is no right and wrong, and that our guilt feelings are the result of someone *telling* us we are bad. Yet I know of no philosopher or individual who has succeeded in convincing himself of that theory for very long."

Janet sighed and slumped in her chair. "I am beginning to see that. I may *think* there is no right and wrong, but I *feel* condemned. I am finding it more and more difficult to live with myself. I even feel alienated from my family." Her eyes were pits of despair as she lowered her voice. "No wonder existentialists dwell on death as the ultimate choice. Nothing else makes sense."

"I have found that some things make a great deal of sense," I said carefully. "If guilt is real—and we seem to agree it is—then it makes more sense to admit it than to deny it."

"So?" Janet's eyebrows were raised slightly.

11

"An admitted guilt isn't hard to define. It is concrete and real, like a debt you know you need to pay."

Janet looked apprehensive, and I smiled. "I know of only one effective way to resolve guilt . . . by forgiveness. I can live with my imperfections today because I know that my debt has been paid by Jesus Christ and I am forgiven."

My listener flinched. "You know I don't agree with that. It's too easy!"

"Not easy," I countered. "It involves the admission that I am not able to handle the guilt question myself, and that my ideas and philosophy are inadequate to explain what is real. It is never easy for me to agree with God that I am helpless and need his forgiveness."

"You seem so sure that God exists," said Janet. "He may be there as an impersonal power behind the universe, but many years ago when I thought of him as personal, I saw him as the judge who declared me guilty in the first place, and accepted me only when I was good. Today I consider a personal relationship with God impossible."

I ached for Janet in her dilemma—facing the reality of guilt, yet unable to accept the total forgiveness of God in Jesus Christ. I know the agony of guilt and few things overwhelm me with such gratitude as the awareness of forgiveness. My guilt is dissolved, and I know I am loved and accepted by God. This recognition always brings an intensified awareness that my relationship with God is intimate and personal. Only a God with personal attributes can forgive. No system of thought or philosophy can do that for us.

I wanted Janet to understand how the first man, Adam, broke his relationship with God through rebellion. Since then, down through history, God has taken the initiative to become reconciled with man by offering forgiveness, acceptance, and love. But there was nothing I could say to convince Janet that God already loved her. I could only attempt to accept her as I knew God had accepted me.

"I think I understand your position," I told her, "and I hope you can understand mine when I say I accept you as a person—

not on the basis of your behavior, but because I choose to accept you as a friend. Can you buy that?"

"Perhaps," Janet shrugged. "But I would not be honest if I didn't tell you I find that hard to believe..."

In Alaska Janet worked as a probation and parole officer, a year-round job that often took her away from home by float-plane to outlying Indian communities. In order to have more time with her family, she decided to return to college in Salem for one more term to earn her teacher's credentials. During those three months, she attended most of our church services, but managed to keep aloof from the people by slipping in late and leaving immediately after a service. In my office she continued to categorize the church as phony.

"They talk about love and acceptance, but I know it only applies to people who fit nicely into the right pattern." As if to prove her point, she deliberately did and said what she called "un-Christian" things. At times I smelled alcohol on her breath, and her attitude seemed to say, "Why don't you send me away so I can prove that you only accept me when I am good."

"Your idea of the church differs from mine," I told her. "I don't see us as a bunch of super-saints who've got it all together and are looking down our noses at those who don't. The Bible and my own experience tell me that the church is simply a group of imperfect people who know they are forgiven and accepted by God and are learning to forgive and accept one another."

"That sounds very nice, Pastor," Janet said softly. "But I know better. Remember, I grew up in the church. What do you think would happen if someone really different wanted to join your group—without conforming to your standards?"

"That would surely put to the test Paul's words to the early church, 'Welcome one another, therefore, as Christ has welcomed you, for the glory of God'" (Rom. 15:7, RSV). I smiled. "That means we ought to be learning to accept each other even in our sins, just as Jesus does."

An almost wistful look crossed Janet's face. "I've still got to be me." There was soberness in her voice. "Your cozy little in-group of a mutual admiration society just isn't my kind of thing."

"You've been open with me and I take that as an expression of trust." I looked directly at her. "Perhaps you ought to let the church know some of the struggles you're going through. They think of you as one of us, you know."

Janet looked startled. "You're right, I'm still on the membership roll . . ." Gazing out the window where a soft drizzle darkened the day, she spoke slowly. "Perhaps I need to say something to the church. I may not know what I am or what I believe, but I know one thing for sure; I'm not a Christian. My life-style and my beliefs differ so drastically from what you people believe that the only decent thing to do is to tell the church and withdraw as a member. . . . I'll feel better when I am not pretending to be something I'm not." Janet looked almost relieved. "Will you call me to the microphone at the end of the sharing service Sunday night? I won't have the courage to speak, otherwise."

She had put me on the spot. The following Sunday evening was a special service. The church would be full, and there would be visitors.

I nodded. "I'll call on you . . . but think it over. Tell the people where you stand, and give them an opportunity to accept that."

The anguish was deep in Janet's eyes. "You are an optimist, Pastor. You believe in the church, but I don't expect to be accepted by them anymore than I expect to be accepted by God."

While the guest speaker delivered his message, I was acutely aware of Janet's pale face in the section of pews to my left. She was obviously determined to carry out her intentions. Her parents sat near the back of the crowded room. They would be deeply hurt by their daughter's action. I wondered what the response of the others would be.

Janet's eyes caught mine, as though she read my thoughts and was asking, "Are you going to let me down, or will you dare to have a lifelong member of the church stand up in front of all these people to say she does not believe in what you stand for?"

Her eyes followed me to the microphone. "Janet Landis has told me she has something to share with us. Will you come up here, Janet?"

There was an expectant silence as she came forward, long-legged in jeans and a loose sweater. Only someone who knew her well would be able to tell that she was under a heavy strain and that her words were carefully chosen.

" . . . I can't pretend any longer. Please accept the withdrawal of my membership from this church."

Quickly she stepped from the platform and walked to the side entrance. As I took her place by the microphone, I was aware that one of our elders had followed her out the door. My heart ached as I spoke: "We have all sensed something of Janet's hurt. I have tried to help her in counseling, and I know something of the struggle she is going through. Now I believe that only as you people respond to her need can she come to understand that God loves her."

In those words, I expressed what I believe is the function of the true church. I believe the church exists here on earth to demonstrate God's love in a way that can be understood and experienced by all who long to know him.

That was the challenge to our church that Sunday evening five years ago when Janet walked out of our building. Until then, most of the people had been unaware of her struggles. Now her pain was visible. Would we be able to respond in a way that would help Janet find the reality she sought so desperately?

Later that evening my wife echoed my thoughts. "I'm glad Janet felt free to share where she stands," Deloris smiled. "She said she wants to come as a visitor. . . . She must have felt reasonably sure we won't reject her. I think that is a good beginning."

Walking out of our auditorium was not the end of Janet's relationship with the church. Her public withdrawal had been a cry for help. Many of the people had understood and would respond, I was sure. In a sense, Janet's relationship with the true church, the family of God, had only begun.

2
You Are
Something Special

There are many ways to communicate how you feel about yourself. Janet Landis, at thirty-five, was a slender, sensitive woman who could have been attractive if she had smiled. Her daily "uniform" was jeans, tennis shoes, a shirt, and a denim jacket. I got the feeling she really didn't like herself.

I've discovered that a surprising number of people feel that way about themselves. I used to think I was the only one. When I was a little boy I wanted to be a great athlete, but I was the skinniest kid on the block, with the biggest nose. The kids occasionally teased me about my nose, and when we played ball I was always the last one to be picked for a team. I still remember how it hurt and how I disliked being me.

Today I feel differently. I even like the way I look; after all, not many people have such a distinctive nose! I am learning to love myself, but that doesn't happen automatically for anyone.

Psychology agrees with the Bible that it is necessary to love ourselves before we can love others. Jesus said: "Love your neighbor *as yourself*." I meet many people who are lonely and feel isolated from others. They very quickly give me the idea that they don't think they are important. "How can anyone love me?" they seem to ask. "I'm so ugly and so dumb." To be a loving person, you first need a healthy self-image.

As a pastor, I believe it is my responsibility to tell people that in God's eyes they are persons of great worth. The good news of the Bible is that God says: "I know you do wrong things, and will always be capable of doing wrong, but don't let that fact overshadow the greater fact that I love you and want you to love yourself."

Self-discovery usually happens in the context of relationships. The first inkling of identity and worth comes to a child when he discovers he has a name and belongs to a family who share that name. His self-image develops further in the day-by-day relationships in the home.

The struggle to find ourselves often becomes an identity crisis in the teen years. Some of us never get it resolved. But there are groups who can help. I remember as a boy on Arlington Avenue in St. Louis, that I belonged to a very exclusive club with my best friend Billy. Our club met in his basement, and my brother Paul, who was three and a half years younger, always tried to join us. To him we were the in-group, because we were older. He would endure all sorts of things to be counted one of us. When Billy's dog Bing spent the night in the basement and did things dogs shouldn't do indoors, we let Paul earn his way into the club by cleaning up after Bing. On those days my little brother looked as though he felt ten feet tall. Alas, his importance was short-lived. When we no longer needed his services, his membership in our club was suspended and his self-esteem plunged.

The in-group system makes us feel special when we're in, but finding ourselves left out is a crushing experience. More of us know how it feels to be left out than to be in.

Only one group can satisfy that deep need inside us to really belong, to be really significant. If you are God's child, by faith in Jesus Christ, you belong to the chosen race that began with Abraham. God called Abraham out of his father's country and said, "Abraham, I have big plans for you. You're going to be especially mine and I'm going to be especially yours." And Abraham became the father of the faithful, the chosen race you and I belong to (1 Peter 2:9). Like Abraham, we are also called individually. "You did not choose me, but I chose you," Jesus said to his disciples (John 15:16, RSV). Peter calls us "a holy nation." A nation is a multitude of people with the same culture. As a holy nation, we are different, set apart for God.

I have a friend whose son was the copilot on *Air Force 1*. Once when our President made a visit to Rumania, this pilot, Captain Sutton, was given the day off. It happened to be Sunday, and as a Christian he wanted very much to be with other Christians. But where do you find other believers when you have just dropped out of the sky into a Communist country?

So Captain Sutton walked out onto the street in front of his hotel, and imagine his excitement when he heard someone whistle the tune, "The Great Physician now is near, the sympathizing Jesus." He followed the sound on the crowded street and caught up with the whistler. Falling into step behind him, the American pilot began to whistle the same tune. Abruptly the man stopped and turned around. His face lit up as he looked into Captain Sutton's eyes. They grabbed each other's arm and did a little dance right there on the sidewalk, pointing to their hearts and to heaven. They recognized each other as God's own people, fellow citizens of the holy nation. And that is something very special.

How does the love of God become real to us? For most of us, the love of God is something very vague until we experience what it means to be accepted by someone who is already in a love relationship with God. That tells me something about the nature and purpose of the true church that I'm still learning more about every day.

One of my early lessons came when I was an administrator in a boarding school in San Diego. When our denomination decided to establish a new mission church in Pacific Beach, I was asked to be its part-time pastor. There were already three Christian and Missionary Alliance churches in the San Diego area, and they formed a steering committee to direct the new project.

The congregation I pastored was made up of six women and a few kids from the neighborhood, and our building was a converted garage which still had the double garage doors and wide driveway.

I felt the need for another man in our group, and asked the

three other pastors if they could spare a lay leader. They all said no, but one of them suggested that I contact a member of his church who lived in our area. "He hasn't been dependable in attendance, and I can never get him to do anything in the church, but you can ask him if you like," he said.

That didn't leave me much choice. The man was a carpenter named George Fagerstrom, who told me right away that he had been recently divorced and was pretty torn up about it. When I said I would appreciate his help in getting a church started in his neighborhood, he looked a little taken aback.

"I'd like to," he responded, "but maybe you can find somebody better qualified. Why don't you pray about it for a week. Then if you still feel you want me, I'll come."

Later George told me that during his personal crisis, he had sensed an urge to serve God in some way. He had heard me speak in his church, and when I later asked him to work with the new mission, he could hardly believe that such an opportunity was being offered. That week I prayed, and when no one else showed up, I went back to tell George I felt God wanted him to come. His response was a firm handshake and a smile that lit up his blue eyes from within.

The next Saturday I had ordered a pile of manure to be dumped on the lot adjoining our building, where I hoped to plant a lawn. Two boys from the Sunday school were there to help when George Fagerstrom showed up. He shook his head and said, "Don, you're a schoolteacher. What are you doing spreading manure?"

"I believe God is going to bring some people together to form a church in this place," I said, "and I want to be a part of it."

Resolutely George waded into the manure pile. "You know, I believe the same thing. Why don't we pray about it together now!"

We knelt right there where our lawn was going to be, and agreed to trust God for the future of his church in Pacific Beach. Then I asked George, "How about helping with the service tomorrow? Would you lead the singing?" He agreed.

Over the next few weeks he pitched in with other things, and we were seeing a lot of each other. I brought my brown bag to eat lunch with George on the construction site, and we met every Tuesday morning at 6:30 to pray for the church. We both believed that real growth and success depended on God.

It didn't take long to realize that if I could have handpicked someone to work closely with me, I would never have picked George. He and I were as opposite as two men could be. I am punctual and like to be organized. George usually showed up late, and didn't like to work on a schedule. But we were friends. George went through some dark and difficult days in his personal life, and spent many hours at our house, talking it out. I recognized, at the root of George's problems, a tremendous sense of guilt. It was very difficult for him to believe that God had forgiven him everything he had ever done wrong. We talked a lot about God's grace, and I told George that I thought of him as a very valuable friend, no matter what he had done.

After many months George finally became convinced that he was forgiven. The realization made a tremendous change in him. He became an avid student of the New Testament and talked endlessly of the joy of being loved undeservedly by God. He and his wife eventually remarried each other.

George often told me that I needed to emphasize the forgiveness and love of God in my sermons rather than preaching about the duties of Christians. I disagreed. In my opinion, it was absolutely necessary that I preach about what God expects of his people. Our church had grown so much that I had gained an associate pastor and we were now in the middle of a building program. The budget had to be met, and in order to be successful as a church, I felt we needed to work harder.

Then one evening, just ten minutes before our annual meeting and election of new church officers, George withdrew his name from the ballot and told me he was leaving us. He and his wife wanted to look for a church with a different slant to the preaching.

"You know how important it is to teach the right doctrine," George told me. "You don't emphasize the grace of God enough."

I took it as a terrible blow, and it was months before I could think about it without feeling hurt. It was hard to resign myself to the fact that George and I were too different to belong to the same church, because I had come to appreciate him as a real friend.

When we ran into each other once at a meeting, I realized how much I had missed him. While our wives hugged, George and I shook hands and told each other it was nice to meet again. I controlled my urge to ask him to come back to us; I didn't want George to think I was pushy. I didn't admit it to myself then, but I am sure I was also afraid he would turn me down.

A couple of weeks later we had a special speaker in our church. George and his wife came to hear him, and it was like homecoming week at school. Everybody hugged and shook hands and said how much they had missed each other. Twice George and his wife came to regular Sunday services before I asked them to our house for coffee and donuts. It was great to be able to talk again and sense that our friendship was still there. But I stifled my urge to say I wished they would come back to stay.

When they were ready to leave, I walked with George out to the car and he said, "Don, do you know what I think is most important in the church?"

"I know you think doctrine is very important . . ."

George shook his head. "Doctrine is important, but there's one thing even more important."

"What is that, George?"

"Love!" He said it quietly. "We feel loved by these people. We can't stay away. We're coming back."

George was not a sentimental man, but there was moisture in his eyes, and I cleared my throat to regain my self-control.

"I've learned something while we've been gone," George smiled. "Your sermons may not be the best, but if the love of God is in the church, the rest will work out sooner or later."

George's return to our fellowship taught me some things I could never have learned any other way. Until then, I had vaguely assumed that people felt more at home in some churches because they liked the preaching. As a pastor, that made me pretty important. But George came back *in spite of* my preaching, because he felt loved and accepted by the people. As far as George was concerned, I was just one of the people who loved him, and that is what counted.

I had always known that love was important in the church, but George showed me something I had not thought much about before: *he loved me by accepting our differences.* His love contained grace, unearned favor. My sermons had not improved so that I could earn George's love; he accepted me the way I was, and I discovered it *felt good* to be accepted that way.

The church needs two legs to walk on: the proclamation of God's love, and the showing of that love in action. Neither works without the other. The evangelical church of which I am a part has most recently come through a period of emphasis on telling the great truths of the Bible. We have been ready to defend that truth, even to the point of fighting among ourselves over some particular points. Through neglecting love, some churches have become cold and people have remained lonely in crowded pews. At the other theological extreme, some churches have emphasized love without Christ as the focal point. Theirs is a mushy love without content or real meaning, and in the end it also leaves us isolated from each other and from God.

Real Christian love begins with God who loves us. Because he loves us, we learn to love each other, and together we love God. It is a continuous three-way relationship in which we are always growing in love. Some of us may be just discovering what it means to be loved. Others are learning to respond and to love even those among us who aren't able to love themselves yet.

When Janet Landis withdrew her membership from our congregation in Salem, she was surprised and even a little annoyed at the response of the people. When she came to see me afterward she asked, "Why don't they just come out and tell me I'm a bad girl who needs to change my ways?" There was a not-so-faint odor of alcohol on her breath. "I've received a stack of cards and letters from people who say they care about my struggles and are praying for me. Not a single one criticizes my action."

"I thought that might happen." I smiled. "You see, you are important to these people."

Janet looked like she wanted to protest; then she shrugged.

"I won't worry about it. When I leave for Alaska, they'll soon forget me."

It didn't happen as she expected. When I saw her several months later, she reported that cards and letters of encouragement continued to reach her in Ketchikan. "I haven't answered anybody." She smiled thinly. "They'll drop me after a while . . ."

"Maybe they won't," I suggested. "Would that make a difference to you?"

"Look, Pastor," her eyes flashed. "I know the church. These people are only trying to win back a lost sheep. They don't care for me as a person. Just wait and see."

One who didn't forget Janet was Carole Meyers, a brown-haired housewife Janet's age. The two had never spoken before Janet publicly withdrew from the church. Carole and her auto mechanic husband, John, were relative newcomers to the church. John was a quiet, reserved fellow. Carole hid her insecurity and shyness behind a bubbly, outgoing facade.

I was a little surprised when Janet mentioned Carole's persistence in letter writing. "If we were at all similar, I could understand her concern," Janet said. "But I'm not her kind of person. We have nothing in common. How can she possibly mean it when she says she cares what happens in my life?" Janet looked exasperated. "But I want you to know I'm as independent as ever. I don't need any friends, and you people don't need me . . ."

When I asked Carole about her correspondence with Janet, she looked a little embarrassed. "It's just something I want to do," she said. "I used to see her in church before, and she looked so lonely I wanted to talk to her—but I didn't know what to say." Carole's blue eyes filled with tears. "When she stood up that night, I really felt bad for her. I remembered standing up there myself and telling everybody how hard it was to accept myself . . . and people showed me they cared. They prayed for me, sent cards, and came to see me. I've never felt so loved . . . if I could only share some of that love with Janet."

"You're doing it," I nodded. "You know you are loved, so you can love someone who doesn't even answer your letters."

Carole's face lit up. "That's what is so neat about it. I've always been afraid of what people thought of me. Even now I wonder if Janet thinks I'm a weirdo or dummy for writing her when she doesn't answer, but it really doesn't matter. I'm learning to reach out to people without worrying about how they respond."

From Janet's occasional short notes to me I learned that the one-way correspondence was continuing. Once she wrote, "I wish Carole Meyers and some of the others in your church would stop reminding me that they and God care. My stack of cards must be two inches thick by now. Remember I'm a rebel and not ready to be tamed . . ."

Occasionally I sent Carole a copy of the part of Janet's letters referring to her. Later she told me:

"Those notes always arrived on a day when I had decided to quit writing to Janet because I was sure she didn't want anything to do with me." She shook her head in amazement. "Every time I think of giving up, someone who has just heard from Janet calls me and says she has mentioned me. Once her husband sent me a card to say how much he appreciates my persistence."

Her eyes were thoughtful. "I know now that God has given me this special relationship with Janet, because he won't let it fade away."

Then one day Carole's face was glowing with a smile. "Guess what!" Her blue eyes glistened with tears. "I had a note from Janet, written on a piece of paper torn from a notebook. She thanked me for making her a macrame plant hanger—isn't it wonderful?"

It was the first crack in Janet's armor. She was beginning to believe that someone really cared.

3
Thank God
for Our Differences!

"I don't think this church needs two Don Bubnas!" My associate pastor's usually mild voice had a sharp edge.

"Why do you say that, Ted?"

"I get the feeling you are trying to make me into another you, and it just won't work."

The strained look on Ted Zabel's open, youthful face told me he was serious, but his words had taken me by surprise. We had been co-workers for a year in the Pacific Beach church. Ted had come to us directly from Bible college, along with his new bride. Edna was a talented musician, and Ted was especially interested in Christian education and youth. The young couple added an exciting new dimension to our growing church. I was impressed with Ted's potential—even if he was a little slow in getting things done, according to my standards. This would soon change, I was sure, as Ted learned my more efficient methods. It was somewhat of a shock to discover that he did not appreciate my coaching.

"I thought one of your reasons for coming here was to learn from a more experienced pastor." I could not conceal my hurt, and Ted nodded in a reaffirming way.

"Of course I came to learn, and I'm excited about working with you because I see you as a strong pastor who is going places."

"Thank you, Ted." His words soothed my wounded feelings.

"But I didn't come because I wanted to be another Don Bubna. I thought that our differences would make us a good team—I thought I would complement your role, and you would not take away from mine . . ."

"Mmmmm." I nodded. Ted had a good point there.

"I share your philosophy and goals for the church," he continued. "But I disagree with your definition of leadership."

"And how do you define my idea of leadership?" My uneasiness had returned. After all, Ted was my twenty-six-year-old assistant, and at thirty-two I had several years experience, both as a school administrator and a pastor. In fact, I considered administration one of my strong points, and the steady growth of our congregation was pretty solid proof that I was a reasonably successful leader.

"I see you trying to lead by getting things done through people your way, and that will only work when the rest of us are robots."

"And how do you feel leadership should function?" There was a defensive edge to my voice.

"It would be far better to get things done through people the way they are most capable of doing them."

In spite of my edginess, I could see some sense in Ted's argument. Perhaps I had been pushing a little hard. "Why haven't you said something about this before?" I covered my unrest with a smile. "We have weekly conferences precisely to talk out any difficulties."

Ted looked awkward. "Usually during our conferences you are upset about something I haven't done on your time schedule, and your idea of 'talking it out' has been to tell me how you do things so that I can do them the same way."

I was getting a little hot under the collar. I had always considered myself a reasonable boss, but obviously Ted had a different impression.

"Has it been that bad?"

"Sometimes," he replied. "That's why I had to speak up before my resentment grew any bigger."

"I appreciate your honesty—I had no idea you felt that way."

I searched for words. "I guess I just wasn't aware of how different we are. I thought you only lacked experience." I made an effort to smile. "Obviously I was wrong. I'll try to do better."

Ted looked immensely relieved. "I didn't mean to hurt you. One of the things I appreciate about working with you is that you are a learner as well as a leader, and I feel that we can learn from each other."

Our conversation was only the first of many like it over the next couple of years. Ted's relaxed, easygoing manner made him popular among the people, and especially so among some that were shy and withdrawn. Around Ted they were comfortable and could open up. The young people liked him, and our Sunday school made great strides under his direction.

I made a deliberate effort not to push him, but when I said it didn't matter how he did some things, as long as they were done on time, he usually received my comment more graciously than I had given it. The sight of his desk piled with unanswered office memos, letters, and unfinished reports had a way of setting off my fuse.

I liked Ted, and a solid friendship had grown between us, but till the day I left for Salem, Oregon, I felt that we could have accomplished a great deal more in Pacific Beach if Ted had been more like me. This feeling gave me a vague uneasiness, as though I was missing a point somewhere. I had been more and more persuaded that the miracle of the church was that people who were vastly different could learn to love one another. If George Fagerstrom and I could work together and experience a bond of love greater than our differences, then surely Ted and I could work things out too.

When I first came to Salem I was just learning to appreciate people who were different from me, but I preferred that they did things my way. I had learned that different people could love one another, but I still saw our differences as a handicap to a smooth relationship.

The first year in Salem seemed to reinforce that impression. I found Oregonians to be different from Southern Californians. My new church was forty years old, and had two hundred attending at the time I arrived. They had indicated that the growth of our Pacific Beach fellowship impressed them, and they wanted me to lead them in a more progressive program in Salem.

Part of my initial effort was to streamline the administration of the church, but some of the more conservative members were reluctant to see any changes in procedure. We agreed on the basic issues of our faith, and this forged a bond of love between us. But the friction over organizational matters, which always occurs in the process of change, made me feel I was bucking a solid wall during some of our business meetings.

Therefore, it was a great relief to get an associate pastor who was a lot like me. He was Paul Gunther, the son of a missionary and pastor who had visited our home when I was a child. His father had pastored the Salem congregation earlier in the church's history and had really laid a sound foundation. Having Paul as an associate was like being joined by a brother. Paul, who wanted to work with a more experienced pastor in preparation for the day when he would pastor his own church, was eager to learn my methods, and I was pleased to see how well we worked together.

At first I was delighted with our similar approach to many issues and the lack of friction between us. Then I began to realize that we were similar not only in our strong points, but in our weak ones as well. There were areas in which I was not too effective, and neither was Paul. Obviously there were disadvantages to a team where the members were too much alike.

Paul was with us for a year and a half until he was called to be the pastor of the Pacific Beach congregation I had formerly served. They loved him from the start, but I had begun to wish for an associate pastor who could do some of the things I couldn't do, and maybe even do them differently than I would have done them. I was talking to my wife about it one day when she looked at me with a direct gaze of her blue eyes and said, "Why don't you come right out and say you wish Ted Zabel was here."

"I guess that's what I'm really thinking, isn't it?" I chuckled in spite of myself. "I'm beginning to appreciate Ted *for* his differences instead of in spite of them. He was just the balance

I needed *because* he was different. It was good for both of us and for the church."

I knew that Ted had returned to seminary, and had a year to go before graduation. We interviewed others to take Paul's place, but the idea of working with Ted stayed in the back of my mind. In January he came to Salem to talk about it. His relaxed, easygoing manner hadn't changed a bit, and the congregation immediately liked him.

"You know, I'd like to work with you, Don," he said, "but it won't be easy. We're as different as ever, and I'll never become a carbon copy of you no matter how hard I try or you might push."

"That's why I want you here," I said. "I need your differences. The church needs them. I can't give them what you have to offer."

The grin was the same. "I need what you are," Ted said. "My ambition is not to become a senior pastor. I want to commit myself to be part of a team that can grow together over the years."

"I appreciate that." I felt strangely moved.

"I think the church can only be built on a long-term commitment to each other," Ted went on. "It is a little like a marriage in that respect. We commit ourselves to love and accept one another and to grow together through some hard times and good times. There can be no backing out when the going gets rough."

"I accept that commitment," I said slowly. "If you sense that God is calling you here, I am prepared to make the same commitment to you." I smiled. "You and I may have different styles and gifts, but we are both committed to Christ and to one another, and I believe that is the heart of the church."

When Ted and I shook hands, I had the distinct feeling that our differences would somehow serve to strengthen the bond of love between us, instead of weakening it as I had once thought. The leadership of our congregation agreed unanimously to wait until Ted's graduation in June to fill the position of minister of Christian education. His coming marked an exciting step for me and for our church fellowship. I was beginning to see that our differences are not meant to separate us, but to draw us together. This is the new and exciting perspective on relationships that only Christianity has to offer.

Ted, who is a capable song leader, likes to remind us that harmony in the church isn't achieved by everybody hitting the same note on the piano. That would only produce a dull, monotonous sound. Instead we are to be like a full orchestra and choir blending in perfect harmony because each is tuned to the same pitch and following the same conductor. Yet to the listening ear, the differences in the instruments and voices remain distinct. A piano isn't supposed to sound like a trumpet, and a soprano doesn't sing like a baritone.

When new members join our church, I like to say: "Our fellowship will never be the same now that you are with us. You will flavor it. You will never be the same—for better or for worse— we will flavor you."

One who flavors our fellowship in a special way is an old man who has been known as something of an oddity in our community for years. Old Tom is in his eighties. He lives alone and likes to stand up whenever we have a time for sharing in the church. He is not always able to keep his thoughts straight, and sometimes rambles on at length. One of our members brought the problem before the executive committee, asking that one of the elders talk to Tom to quiet him down. Brad Coleman, a young attorney on the committee, objected. "If our church doesn't have room for the old Toms, we're in the wrong kind of church!"

Not long ago, a couple of young bachelors took Tom out for Sunday dinner and afterwards referred to their time together as "really neat!" When we held a special service for a young woman who left our congregation to be a missionary, old Tom stood up to say, "That young lady will make a good missionary; she always talks to me." I thought his comment said a great deal about what it means for a lonely old man to belong to the family of God.

One of our most unique members is Peter, who is in his forties but has the mentality of a small child. He lives only a few blocks from our building, in a sheltered care home. Week after week Peter beams on us with his smile, and his presence has come to mean much to a number of people. We know that Peter understands his special relationship to God and to us. One morning in my Sunday school class he responded to a question about God, saying, "He is alive!" The big smile on Peter's face told us all that he was personally acquainted with the living Christ. Glancing around the crowded room, I saw the moist eyes and warm smiles of Christians who regarded Peter as their brother.

Children have a special love for him, and are eager to sit beside him in the pew during the service. If someone becomes a little rowdy, Peter scolds the person mildly, and he immediately quiets down. Many have told me how Peter's openness and warm familiarity with his many friends in the church speak to them in a special way of the diversity and love of God's family. God uses Peter to show us his love in ways no one else could.

Then there is Bobby, an eight-year-old who was adopted by a family in the church. Bobby, an autistic child, had been in a school for retarded children, where he became convinced that he could never learn.

From the time of his arrival in the Duarte household, Bobby often spoke with great concern about becoming "a big man." "A big man," to Bobby, was someone who could read and count.

One day, after playing with Peter in the yard, Bobby seemed anxious for his new friend. "Peter won't ever be a big man, because he can't read or count," Bobby said, his eyes riveted on his father's face.

"Peter is an adult," Mr. Duarte explained, "but he cannot learn. He is retarded."

"Does God love him?"

"Yes, Bobby, God loves him just as he is." Bobby's face lit up, and his father continued, "God loves you and wants you to do as much with your ability as Peter has done with his."

Bobby stood in deep thought; then he smiled. "I can learn."

Mr. Duarte nodded. "That's right, son, you can." He watched Bobby skip happily out the door. A small miracle had happened. Peter had been God's special messenger to show Bobby that he could learn. This was a turning point in Bobby's life.

Our church would be less of a church without people as different as Ted and I, or without Peter, old Tom, little Bobby, and every one of the varied company that makes up the body of Christ in Salem.

Once a man came to me for counseling and I asked him, "What do you think God is like?" He hesitated for a moment, then said, "All I know about him is that he must be like Jesus." God showed himself in Jesus who walked this earth, touching lives, communicating God's love to men. Paul tells us that God is revealing himself in a second body of Christ, the church.

"Now here is what I am trying to say: All of you together are the one body of Christ and each one of you is a separate and necessary part of it" (1 Cor. 12:27, TLB).

God wants to reveal himself in our lives—collectively. The marvel of the body is its diversity. Have you ever looked at a human infant and been amazed by the perfection of all the parts functioning together? Everything is there, the little fingers, the eyes, the ears, the mouth, the little button nose, and ten pink toes. Similarly, to see God in the church, the world needs to observe the diversities of its parts and marvel at how they fit together.

One of our members is a high school teacher named Mary Ellen Travis. She was in her fifties when she first came to visit our church. Now that her son is dead, we are her only family and she says about us: "I've never seen such a diversified group of people: they're from every walk of life and different levels of prosperity. Professionals, working people, farmers, and educators. Some who have four or five cars and some who have only a bicycle. The old and the very young, those who are hurting, those who are seeking, and those who are in various stages of finding themselves and God. It is tremendous. It is not what you have or what you are that counts, but who you love."

The phrase "body of Christ" implies multiplicity and interdependence. We need each other because we are different, and the greater the differences, the greater the potential there is for the church itself to experience the many facets of God's love. God expresses his love and his nature in Peter and in Tom, and in each of us a little differently. The greater our diversity, the more we see his love unfolding among us, and the more we are a witness to the world.

One of the fellows in my Sunday school class made this statement one morning: "I've been thinking a lot this week about how God wants to make himself known to the world. We as his people are what makes him credible. God uses us to show the world who he really is—it's almost frightening!"

I've felt that way myself sometimes. It is exciting—and almost frightening, but God is not narrowly defined. Our diversity as his people is meant to illustrate the greatness of his love. That can only happen when we come to appreciate each other *for* our differences instead of in spite of them.

4
Koinonia—
The Real Thing

I don't like criticism, but I am learning that critics often say things I need to hear. Several years ago a national church leader visited a meeting held by my denomination. He had been raised in a church with a theology similar to ours, but had left it as a young man. His mother, who still belonged to that church, frequently wrote him asking, "Son, when are you coming back to the true faith?"

He told us: "In the same letter she tells me how one group in the church still won't associate with another. There are schisms and a bitterness that has lasted for years...that's what my mother wants me to return to!"

His remarks probably hurt more than anything I ever heard said about the church, yet I needed to hear them. As I travel today I hear his words echoed, not by critics outside the church, but by those on the inside. In our own congregation in Salem, we have a number of outspoken people who have been turned off by the organized church. They label it cold, unfriendly, and hypocritical. They say, "You hear talk about Christian love—but you don't feel it."

Sadly, there is a measure of truth in that. The church often appears cold and impersonal. It is especially tragic because it means we are not being the true church. We are missing what Jesus said would be the mark of the Christians, their love for one another.

Loving difficult people isn't "doing what comes naturally." I fail miserably even if I drum up all my willpower. Our only hope is something the Greeks called *koinonia*. The word appears eighteen times in the New Testament, describing a special relationship in the Holy Spirit between man and God and man and other men. It means that my relationship with God and with other Christians is interwoven. My relationship with God is affected by how I get along with my brothers and sisters in the church, and my love for them depends on my relationship with God. I can't really love God without loving other Christians, or the other way around.

Paul wrote to the Corinthians: "The grace of the Lord Jesus Christ, and the love of God, and the fellowship [*koinonia*] of the Holy Spirit, be with you all" (2 Cor. 13:14, NASB). Paul speaks here of a fellowship with God through the Holy Spirit. This is God wanting to share with us his mercy and grace, his very nature and attributes, through the Holy Spirit. That is how *koinonia* begins; by God sharing with man.

The second aspect of this sharing is between men. In Philippians 2:1 Paul speaks of "the fellowship [koinonia] of the Spirit." The context shows that this has to do with our fellowship among Christians. *Koinonia* with God and with one another must be in operation together. It is our fellowship with God that supplies the content for real fellowship with one another.

In recent years there has been much talk about a Holy Spirit movement in the church, and the word *koinonia* has sometimes been used to describe a sharing of spiritual experiences. The Greek word implies something more practical than mystical. It simply says that through the Holy Spirit I have access to an intimate fellowship with God and with my Christian brothers and sisters.

I find it helpful once in a while to be reminded of how the early church began. Two thousand years ago, God chose to reveal himself in the second person of the Trinity, Jesus Christ. He came as a man, was born, wrapped in swaddling clothes, and laid in a manger. Before he died he told his disciples: "I will come again in the person of the Holy Spirit."

In the second chapter of Acts we have the account of the first local church in the New Testament. The core of the group had been with Jesus for three and a half years. They had experienced walking and working and eating, sharing their lives with Christ. Suddenly Jesus was torn from their midst through the terrible experience of the crucifixion, and then marvelously restored through the resurrection. But then forty days later he left them by ascending to the Father in heaven, and told the disciples to wait for the Comforter, the Holy Spirit, to come. On Pentecost, in the person of the Holy Spirit, Jesus came again, indwelling and filling them, so that they might have *koinonia* with God and with each other.

Before, he was *with* them; now he is *in* them. They were keenly aware of his presence. Peter talked about it on the day of Pentecost—how Jesus now was Master and Lord of their lives. Because they felt it individually, they joined themselves together. *Koinonia* between them began when they recognized their *koinonia* with God through the Holy Spirit.

To maintain and nurture the *koinonia* in the church, Paul later commanded the Christians to keep on being filled with the Holy Spirit: "Don't drink too much wine, for many evils lie along that path; be filled instead with the Holy Spirit, and controlled by him" (Eph. 5:18, TLB).

Being filled with the Holy Spirit was a prerequisite for the *koinonia* relationship. Today there is much confusion about what it means to be filled with the Holy Spirit and what the evidence of it should be. Often it is associated with a mystical experience and the ability to praise God, especially in another tongue. Speaking in tongues is listed as a gift of the Holy Spirit, but in connection with the command to be filled with the Spirit, Paul does not mention gifts as evidence. In fact, on another occasion he wrote a rather stern letter to the Christians at Corinth who had been baptized in the Holy Spirit. They exhibited the gifts of the Holy Spirit in their church, but there was obviously a great lack of *koinonia*. They were not filled with the Spirit (1 Cor. 3:1-4). The Greek verb "to be filled" is used in a continuous sense that doesn't exist in our English language. It means "keep on being filled." Paul contrasts it with the experience of being drunk, because in order to stay drunk a man has to keep on drinking.

If being filled with the Spirit is not just a mystical experience, how does it happen? Jesus explained it quite simply to his followers on the last day of the Feast of Tabernacles, a Jewish festival commemorating the entrance into the Promised Land after the Israelites had wandered in the wilderness for forty years.

With his disciples, Jesus was watching the colorful procession led by a priest who carried a golden pitcher from the Temple to the Pool of Siloam. There the pitcher was filled with water and the procession returned to the Temple, where the water was poured out on the west side of the altar. Most Jewish religious rituals had two functions: to remind the people of something God had done for them in the past, and also of something he had promised through the prophets for the future. The pouring out of the water commemorated how God had miraculously provided water during the wilderness wanderings, and also the future outpouring of the Holy Spirit promised by Joel.

That morning on the last Feast of Tabernacles before his crucifixion, Jesus stood up to proclaim loudly that he himself would give water to those who came to him—water to drink, and water to flow from them to others. John recorded the event in his Gospel and explained that Jesus was referring to the Holy Spirit.

In the original Greek the meaning is clearer because the words of Jesus are recorded in the same continuous tense Paul used in commanding us to keep being filled with the Holy Spirit. Jesus said: "If any man is [continually] thirsty, let him [continually] come to Me and [continually] drink. He who [continually] believes in Me . . . from his innermost being shall [continually] flow rivers of living water" (John 7:37, 38, NASB).

It isn't enough to come to Jesus once. We are to keep coming to drink because we keep thirsting, and so we keep on being filled with the Holy Spirit, and the evidence of it keeps flowing from our lives to others.

Spirit-filled Christians should be talking with one another, sharing our life in Christ. We should be praising and worshiping God together. We should always be grateful, and we should be honoring Christ by considering the needs of others before our own. Another word for this is *koinonia*.

We cannot claim the fullness of the Holy Spirit, however deep or intimate our communion with God may seem, if we don't have fellowship with one another. If *koinonia* is lacking in the church, we are not Spirit-filled Christians. We may have spiritual experiences, and exercise spiritual gifts, but we do not have that most obvious fruit of the Spirit-filled life—love for one another (1 John 4:7-10).

Koinonia is a love relationship, but the presence of the Holy Spirit in the church doesn't mean we automatically love one another. When I first came to Salem I wrote the two words LOVE and UNITY on the chalkboard and asked the congregation to join me in praying that our relationships as a church would be marked by those two qualities. Eunice Thompson, one of our church secretaries, likes to remind me of that first prayer meeting.

"I had never seen those words on a prayer request before," she says. "But ever since, it seems we've been talking and praying about love and unity morning, noon, and night."

Love and unity can't be produced by us. They are given to the church by the Holy Spirit, but we must maintain and nurture them. When we do, we have *koinonia*.

The word *koinonia* in the Greek also implies a deliberate, deep commitment. It was commonly used to refer to a business partnership or a marriage. The lives and fortunes of business partners were deeply linked together. That was *koinonia*. So was the enduring commitment of a man and a woman in marriage.

In our day and culture many people shy away from deep commitments. An increasing number of couples live together without a marriage license. Some say it is because they expect their feelings to one day cool off, and they don't want to make any promises they can't keep.

I believe our fear of deep commitments to one another stems from a misunderstanding of what a commitment should be based on. If my promise to love my wife forever is based on the hope that I will always have sweet romantic feelings for her, I might not dare commit myself for "as long as we both shall live." Feelings are somewhat beyond my control, and God only knows how I'll feel twenty years from now. If marriage is only based on romantic feelings, I can understand the young couples who hesitate to make lifelong commitments, particularly in view of the phenomenal rise in the divorce rate. After all, we must assume that all the hundreds of thousands of couples who painfully part in the divorce courts once had beautiful feelings for one another and were certain their love would never end.

Some couples rewrite the marriage agreement to what they consider to express a more realistic and honest commitment: to be true to one another "as long as our love shall last." What they obviously mean is: "as long as our beautiful feelings for one another shall last." It is unfortunate that the only word we have for love has such a limited meaning in daily usage. The Greeks had several words to express different aspects of the thing we simply translate "love."

Jesus could not have meant "beautiful feelings" when he spoke of loving our enemies and loving one another in our families and in the church, because he made it a command. The word Jesus used was *agape*, and if you and I had been Greek-speaking Christians in the first century, we would immediately have known that Jesus was talking about an act of our will, not a state of our emotions. There were other words to describe warm, affectionate feelings of friendship, deep and tender family relationships or strong romantic attraction. The command to practice *agape* love for someone went beyond all the others and would last even when the others had faded or failed.

When we experience being loved that way by God and by someone who loves him, it becomes possible for us to also love with an *agape* love. "We love because he first loved us," wrote the Apostle John. The word he used was *agape*. It is a level of love more mature than the warm, affectionate feelings we had for those who first loved us. It means daring to commit ourselves to love the unlovable no matter what it may cost or how they respond.

This kind of commitment is never easy, but with the *koinonia* of the Holy Spirit it is no longer impossible. The ability to love the unlovable isn't mine, but when I make the decision to *will* to love, Jesus supplies the ability through the Holy Spirit.

Paul wrote: "Be kind to each other, tenderhearted, forgiving one another, just as God has forgiven you because you belong to Christ" (Eph. 4:32, TLB). One of the most incredible examples of this kind of *agape* love took place in our church not long ago.

A boy had been killed in a car accident, and following the funeral his parents greeted those of us who had come to share this hour with them. Among the people was the man who had driven the vehicle that took their son's life. He had been to their home, but now he and his wife came once more to express their grief.

"Can you ever forgive me, can you ever forgive me, can you ever forgive me?" he repeated. Hopeless tears coursed down the man's face.

Quietly the parents of the dead boy responded, "We have forgiven you. It is well."

Such is the portrait of love God wants the world to see in the church: *koinonia* with God and each other.

I believe that when we experience the forgiveness and love of God and extend it to one another, we are actually foretasting a little bit of heaven. We are told that heaven is a real place and that the New Jerusalem will have streets of gold and pearly gates. But I think heaven is more than a place. I believe the essence of it is *koinonia*, an ever-widening relationship with God and one another. I can get tired of sight-seeing, but I never get tired of growing relationships. I've heard people say, in response to real *koinonia*, "If it can be like this on earth, what is it going to be like in heaven?"

Getting to know God and each other is a lifetime experience, and to think that we will continue in a deepening love for one another throughout eternity is exciting. Real *koinonia* is what Jesus had with the Father, and just before his crucifixion he prayed for his followers:

"My prayer for all of them is that they will be of one heart and mind, just as you and I are, Father—that as you are in me and I am in you, so they will be in us, and the world will believe you sent me" (John 17:21, TLB).

He is saying "Father, just as you and I have this very unique unity and fellowship, I want the disciples to have the same thing with us." *Koinonia* is the answer to Jesus' prayer that we are to be one with him and with one another. When *koinonia* exists in the church, it allows the church to be the caring, loving community it was meant to be: the portrait of love God wants the world to see.

An elderly man in our fellowship said the other day, "I've been a Christian for over thirty-nine years, but only recently have I begun to discover what God's love really means. Before it was always a vague thing. Now it is becoming personal and real as I sense it in our relationships in the church."

A young housewife who is a newcomer to our fellowship, said, "The love is something you feel the minute you walk through the door—it is like a tasty piece of candy. Once you've tasted it, you want more."

Koinonia is an observable love. When it is in the church, it draws people more effectively than any advertising. Several years ago we had an unusual amount of publicity in the local newspaper. Our missionary convention was the subject of several stories, and we happened to be featured as the church of the week. To buy that much advertising space would have cost a small fortune.

The following Sunday evening we had ten or twelve visitors. I asked if they had seen the write-ups about us in the paper. None of them had. They came because they had a friend in our congregation. Real *koinonia* is almost irresistible to those who are looking for God and reality.

One of the first persons I met in Salem was the son of one of our most faithful members. The son was a successful businessman, something of a loner who attended the church and gave to the general fund, but was not what you would call an enthusiastic member. Every so often he would make a point of telling me what he thought was wrong with the institutional church. I did not agree with him, but I could understand his viewpoint and we were friends.

Just a couple of years ago, he called and asked to meet with our staff. He told us: "I've been offering my money to you, but never the real me. Now I see that some significant things are happening in the relationships of this church, and I wonder if there is a place for a guy like me."

For eleven years he had watched from the sidelines. Now he had caught the flavor of real *koinonia* and wanted to make a commitment of himself as well as of his money.

In my files is a note from a young Filipino who attended our church for several months while visiting Salem. He was a Christian who had great problems in accepting the organized church.

He wrote: "You have made a deep impression in my life because of the way the love of Christ and his acceptance pervades your life. I could sense it from the first day I entered your church building. I have had a lot of hangups about the whole of 'conservative theology,' but my stay with you proved me wrong. I found how Jesus Christ can make a life *life* regardless of the difference in all these theologies. I especially thank you for the human touch in your life-style, for teaching me truth, and for sharing with me Jesus Christ in a way I have never experienced before..."

That young man tasted *koinonia*—the real thing—and the taste made him hungry for the continuing relationship with God and man.

5
Let's Eat Together!

For as long as I can remember, I have had the idea that eating with people is a great way to make friends. Some of my happiest memories from childhood are of the steady stream of guests at our table.

We lived in a section of St. Louis that was far from affluent. My dad was a maintenance man and we lived in what was called "three straight rooms." You stepped through the front door into the living room and walked through the bedroom to the kitchen. Later we were able to rent an additional room upstairs for a boys' bedroom, but frequently we slept on the floor because visitors had our beds.

At a seminar not long ago, a man greeted me warmly and said, "Hey, don't you remember me? I stayed in your home five weekends in a row when I was in the service in 1945. A buddy in my home church in Philadelphia had told me that if I ever came to St. Louis, I should go to the Bubnas' because they would take care of me." He shook my hand heartily. "I'll never forget your parents' hospitality."

Mom and Dad's deep commitment to hospitality was probably one of their greatest gifts to their three sons. Although poor by many standards, they enthusiastically offered food and a bed to those they felt needed it. Many Saturdays during World War II I remember Mom and Dad going downtown to bring home as many as four servicemen who were on leave in a strange city. Whenever our church had a visiting pastor or missionary, he came to our house for dinner.

We boys relished the flavor these folks brought, and got the impression early that serving Christ was the most exciting activity in the world. Had it not brought all these different people to our home? Hospitality, more than any other single influence in our youth, probably directed each of us brothers toward our future calling as pastors.

It is nothing new that hospitality is important in human relationships. Eating together always tends to help us break down barriers and promotes a greater intimacy. A man who is serious about courting a woman invites her out for a candlelit dinner. Salesmen take their clients to lunch, and statesmen settle affairs of nations at banquet tables.

The first sign that a friendship is developing is often an invitation to continue talking over a cup of coffee and donuts. A luncheon engagement may follow, and then a dinner date with husbands and wives included. Much later—if all signals are clear —comes an invitation to a snack or a meal at home. Most societies are more formal than our North American culture, but we all share a basic hesitancy to ask a stranger into our home.

In the Bible we find that hospitality and the simple act of eating together played a significant part in spreading God's love to the world. If we were to remove from the New Testament the instances of Jesus eating with someone, we would lose a substantial part of his teachings.

I don't think it is incidental that the writers recorded the fact that Jesus was sharing a meal with someone while teaching some of the great truths he had come to bring us. To the Jew, eating with someone was a sign of acceptance and intimacy. What simpler way to demonstrate that God loves and accepts all men, and offers them an intimate relationship?

Few things enraged the Jewish religious leaders as much as Jesus' habit of eating with all kinds of people. In those days, inns and public eating places were few, so to share a meal with someone usually meant you went to his house or he came to yours. When Jesus accepted invitations to go to the homes of tax collectors as well as Pharisees, his critics were furious. Luke records that "the Pharisees and scribes began to grumble, saying, This man receives sinners and eats with them" (Luke 15:2, NASB). In response, Jesus told them the stories of the lost coin, the lost sheep, and the runaway son. When that which has been lost is found, there is great rejoicing, and "in the same way . . . there is joy in the presence of the angels of God over one sinner who repents." When the runaway son returned home to his father, they celebrated the reconciliation by eating a feast together.

Jesus was letting his critics know that eating with sinners was his way of seeking the lost and celebrating their coming to him.

During the years of his earthly ministry, Jesus did not maintain a household of his own. So we know he often must have accepted hospitality in homes throughout the regions where he traveled. When he sent his disciples out to the lost sheep of Israel, to announce that the Kingdom of God was at hand, he instructed them to bring neither food nor money (Mark 6:8, 9). "And don't hesitate to accept hospitality," he told them, "for the workman is worthy of his wages!" (Luke 10:7, TLB).

The disciples were to depend on hospitality, and the willingness of others to house and feed them was to be a sign of a home that was open to receive him who had sent them. If they were not welcomed, Jesus instructed them to withhold their blessing from any home that did not welcome them, and to shake the dust of that place from their feet as they left. "Truly, the wicked cities of Sodom and Gomorrah will be better off at Judgment Day than they" (Matt. 10:13, TLB).

I preached one of my first sermons in Salem on the subject of eating with sinners as a biblical strategy for spreading Christianity. The congregation had sent word before I arrived that they were interested in evangelism as a means of church growth. My idea of evangelism, as developed over several years in Pacific Beach, was to follow the example of Jesus, who touched people's lives by becoming their friend and loving them. A good way to begin this friendship evangelism, I suggested, was to share a meal with someone who was a stranger to Jesus Christ and his church.

The sermon was very well received. Several people shook my hand and said, "Great idea, just what we need!" But I didn't notice that anyone did much about it. I asked the men who served on the various committees to pray with me and give themselves to hospitality. Then I preached again on friendship as a tool in introducing people to God. The second sermon was even better received than the first.

Encouraged, I asked around if anyone had found opportunities to share their life and faith, perhaps while entertaining at home or taking someone out for lunch. My questions were met mostly by silence. Those who did respond, I suspected of having done that kind of thing all along.

There appeared to be general agreement in the church that touching people for Christ by being their friend was a biblical principle of evangelism. The good news that God loves us is meant to be communicated to the whole world. That topic crept into my sermons frequently, simply because I found it echoed again and again in the pages of my Bible.

Yet it was discouraging that so little seemed to come of it. Why, when we as Christians enthusiastically believed in spreading the Good News, did we find it so difficult to break out of the ingrown pattern of most congregations? Increasingly I pondered the reasons for our reluctance to get involved with strangers who might be potential friends—and fellow believers.

This reluctance was an obstacle in my own life as well. Establishing new relationships was often a difficult thing, and entertaining at home always caused a certain amount of tension. My wife was a pastor's daughter and had learned to cope with the extra responsibility of hospitality that seems to fall on a pastor's wife, yet I knew that having guests was a struggle for her.

"It's because I want everything to be just right!" she retorted one afternoon when I asked her why she was making such a fuss over company for dinner. I had come home to find her rushing around the house picking up children's toys, dusting the furniture, setting the table, and tending the roast in the oven. Now she looked in quiet resignation at the couch where the stuffing was spilling out, and our threadbare rug where a hole was growing more noticeable every time the children stumbled over it.

"They'll just have to take us as we are," she shrugged. "I can't hide the condition of our furniture."

"They won't care," I said absent-mindedly. "It's the fellowship that matters, not what our house looks like."

"I *know* that!" Dee's voice was a shade higher than normal. "But I still *feel* uptight, and I'm sure most of the women in the world feel the same when *their* house is a mess and company is due in an hour!"

I stubbornly chose to ignore the hint that I help with the last-minute preparations. It had been a hard day at the office, I reasoned, and I needed a moment's quiet before evening. I thought my only responsibility was to insure an evening of pleasant and meaningful fellowship with our guests. Dee could handle the practical aspects of feeding and putting three small children to bed, and have the table ready and waiting for our guests. As usual she would do a superb job (no thanks to me), even if the effort left her exhausted the next day.

Such was the price of modern-day hospitality, I mused as I sipped my tea. No wonder our affluent society did less of it than when we had fewer belongings to worry over and a simpler fare to share.

Although I had rationalized my position and shrugged off Dee's remarks that day, they returned to me with new intensity as I listened more carefully to conversations in the church. If the other men helped as little as I did, it was no wonder that most women felt uptight about entertaining. And perhaps they did not invite others to their homes because they feared criticism if the meal or the furniture was less than splendid.

If so, perhaps we needed to examine the biblical record of hospitality in the early church to see what prompted the first Christians to share responsibilities and possessions and to open their homes to one another. I feared that the reluctance to practice hospitality in our present-day church was not just an attitude toward strangers, but also toward other Christians who were not of our immediate group or clique.

In the Book of Acts, which gives the first glimpse of the brand new church, I read that the members continued "breaking bread from house to house . . . taking their meals together with gladness" (Acts 2:46, NASB). The early Christians didn't come together to show off new furniture or impress each other with their cooking. "They shared all things in common," said the Bible, and eating together was the most effective way to show love and acceptance, and to nurture their new *koinonia* relationship.

Hospitality, although an effective way to reach strangers with the news of God's love, was first of all to be extended to other Christians, and not just as a pleasant convenience. Paul used strong words when he *commanded* the new believers to "practice hospitality." The Greek word means "pursue the practice of hospitality." Go after it—don't wait till you're asked to entertain someone. The command occurs several times, in fact more often than the often-quoted "Great Commission" to preach the gospel to the world.

Peter wrote: "Practice hospitality to one another—that is of the household of faith. (Be hospitable, that is be a lover of strangers, with brotherly affection for the unknown guests, the foreigners, the poor and all others who come your way who are of Christ's body.) And (in each instance) do it ungrudgingly ... without complaining, but as representing Him" (1 Pet. 4:9, Amplified Bible).

Hospitality in the early church was designed for Christians to put into practice the command to love one another. It meant you ate with and invited to your home people you had never associated with before, to demonstrate to them and to the world that now you are brothers.

No wonder the practice of hospitality was made a qualification for men who were to hold leadership positions in the church. With some concern I noticed that the requirement was for the *man* to be "hospitable" (Titus 1:8; 1 Tim. 3:2), not just his wife. I began to realize that I was meant to go beyond inviting the guests and then sitting in the living room to entertain them, while Dee did the rest. I could no longer sit back and sip tea while she worked.

Obviously hospitality was considered far more important in the early church than it is in our day. It began to occur to me that our neglect of it had more serious implications than I had once thought. A lack of hospitality probably contributed significantly to the absence of *koinonia* fellowship in the church. Little wonder that we found it hard to be hospitable to strangers —we had not yet learned the basics of practicing it among ourselves.

It was one thing to diagnose where we were, another to prescribe a cure. I had gone to the Oregon coast for a three-day study break when the thought came to me, Why not take an open survey in the church to discover our attitudes toward and practices of hospitality? I would share the findings with the congregation and that would form a springboard for a study of hospitality in the early church.

One Sunday evening, as the people came to the service, they were handed a sheet with multiple choice questions. No one was required to sign the form. The ushers collected them, and I read the results from the pulpit. The questions went like this:

1. I entertain fellow Christians in our home (check the one that fits):
   a. frequently (2 or 3 times a month)
   b. regularly (about once a month)
   c. occasionally (5-10 times a year)
   d. rarely (4 or less times a year)
   e. almost never

2. Of those I do entertain, what percent are other than my close friends? (Circle one.)
   a. 10%
   b. 25%
   c. 50%
   d. 75%
   e. _____

3. The reason I don't entertain more is (check all answers that apply):
   a. we are busy
   b. it costs a lot
   c. our home furnishings are too modest/or inadequate
   d. having guests frightens me
   e. I get too tense and exhausted getting the house cleaned and the food prepared, etc.

The answers showed that Dee and I were no exceptions. The majority of the congregation rarely entertained, and those who did seldom invited people who weren't close friends already. (If I had not been a pastor, our pattern of hospitality would most likely have fallen with the majority.)

The reasons most often checked for not entertaining were: "having guests frightens me," and "our home furnishings are too modest/or inadequate."

With the facts out in the open, most people were surprised and relieved to discover that almost everybody felt the same way. Since then I have taken similar surveys in other churches and groups, and found that we in Salem are not atypical.

That evening I shared with the congregation what I had learned about hospitality in the early church. What were our reasons for not obeying the biblical command? To be ashamed of our furniture or afraid of serving an inadequate meal can best be described as pride, and in the Bible pride is not considered a valid excuse—it is simply called sin.

We have been conditioned by our culture to judge people by what they own, and expect others to judge us the same way. We put things before people when we say, "Wait until we get the new drapes up, then we'll have people in for a meal." That kind of entertaining erects barriers between us, and hides our humanness.

Christian hospitality says: "We don't have much furniture, but we'd like to have you come. We don't have elegant food, but we can whip up some pancakes. We'd like you to see us the way we are, so come as you are. We'll get to know each other better."

Christian hospitality is an act of receiving and entertaining others without expectation of reward, but with kindness and consideration. It is an act of saying, "I love you."

Now that we had put it into words, we began to work on a strategy to develop hospitality in the church in Salem. I saw the pastor's role as threefold:

1. Continue to teach about the biblical principle of hospitality from the pulpit.
2. Practice it myself

3. Provide opportunities for training and practice in the church.

A first step was to reduce all regular evening activities related to the church to three nights a week. With something going on every night, our most enthusiastic members had little time for their families, and none to entertain guests. That rule still stands, and applies to pastors and the rest of the staff as well.

In my personal schedule, I began to put more emphasis on having lunch or breakfast with one or several men, getting to know them better and encouraging them to adopt the same practice with others. My wife developed a similar pattern of having lunch with other women.

At home, we began having people over at least three or four times a month. Dee was relieved to find me more willing to share the responsibility for the preparation, serving, and cleanup stages of entertaining. She had always taken pride in preparing the entire meal by herself. Now she began to see that her guests often felt more comfortable if they were allowed to bring a dish. Gradually our entertaining at home evolved into a multipurpose happening. Among our guests are usually some who are new in our fellowship, as well as some who are in "hospitality training." Quite often we call someone in that group to say: "We know you are working on practicing hospitality; how about coming over to meet some new people we're having in for dinner?"

If we're having a crowd, we don't hesitate to ask someone to help in the kitchen, with serving or with the cleanup.

We learned early that it is important to keep it simple. Rather than having people for a complete meal, we often invite them to share a casual snack. We try to make it clear that the emphasis is on the fellowship, not the food.

Soon after our survey on hospitality, we began opening several homes for a friendship hour once a month after our Sunday evening service. The first time we did it, one of the hostesses put on a beautiful spread of fancy foods. No one thought they could live up to that, so others were reluctant to open their homes. Then we made a firm rule for everyone to serve only what you can hold in a napkin with one hand while you hold your paper cup with coffee or punch in the other. Standard fare is donuts, cookies, a piece of cake, or popcorn.

Now that we have acquired a new couch and wall-to-wall carpeting in our home, we have discovered this is not an advantage. Our guests, especially young couples with small children, now are more self-conscious about their own furniture with the stuffing coming out. We tell them that entertaining without fancy furniture is a definite plus, because people relax more and find it easier to return your hospitality.

We began with four or five homes for each friendship hour. Today there are a dozen or more, and we have found that a one bedroom apartment or small mobile home is just as convenient as something larger. In fact, it is an advantage when there are not enough chairs for everybody. It makes for better circulation among the groups. Sitting on the floor is also less formal.

Our deacons are responsible for the arrangements, recruiting host-homes in different parts of the city. When people arrive for the Sunday evening service, a deacon and his wife greet them at the door with a printed address card informing them which family will entertain them that evening.

The host-homes are not announced in the bulletin, because we discovered that people tend to choose the home of a close friend. One of the purposes of the friendship hour is to encourage people to move beyond their own group.

A deacon with his family is in attendance at each open home. He makes an effort to see that everyone is introduced and attempts to tune into people's interests and needs, guiding the conversation from baseball or the weather to a more meaningful sharing. This he can do by asking questions or sharing something from his own Christian experience. If I haven't been preaching at the service, I find it easy to ask, "What did you get out of the service today?" Another ice breaker is, "What have you been learning about the Christian life since coming to our church?"

The structured opportunities of the friendship hour have been stepping-stones to a wider circle of friends and greater self-confidence for many who have been timid or shy. One young couple moved to Salem from Canada. Dick Faith was the manager of a printing plant. He and his wife Donna had two small children. Donna was unusually shy, and when Dick felt that they should enter the mission field as full-time Christian workers, Donna was at first fearful.

They were home on leave from Africa not long ago, and Donna told us that hospitality was an important part of their ministry in a foreign country. "It was one of the things that meant so much to us here in Salem," she said. "When we first came here, we were invited to someone's home right away, and the invitations kept on coming as long as we were here. That helped more than anything to overcome my fear of people."

Hospitality is a two-way street. It has to be accepted as well as offered. Some people are too busy or too tired, or afraid to go to a friendship hour, but most people who don't go are afraid of the risk of meeting new people. In pursuing hospitality, we have learned that it requires taking some risks.

When we first began to emphasize hospitality, there were some who grasped the idea eagerly. They began to invite others home for dinner every Sunday after church. Jim Thompson was chairman of our elders and his wife, Eunice, was church secretary. One day Jim came to me and said, "Don, we invited some visitors for dinner, but they hemmed and hawed and didn't come." He smiled a little. "Looks like we scared them away; they haven't been back since. Maybe you ought to preach on accepting hospitality as well as offering it."

It was a point I had not considered. Often it is easier for people to give than to receive. Now we talk about both sides of hospitality. Many of us have discovered that it becomes more meaningful to give when we learn to receive more gracefully.

The structured happenings encourage many to practice hospitality on their own. A number of people now make it a habit to invite others to a donut shop or home for a snack after services. Our young singles or others who live alone are regularly included in such get-togethers. Some of our families with small children seem to have "adopted" sets of "aunts," "uncles," "grandmas," or "grandpas" for special holiday celebrations or other occasions when those who live alone are the loneliest.

Mary Ellen Travis, the high school teacher who joined our church family when she was in her early fifties, describes herself as a private person who likes to be alone. But often she joins one of the families who seem to count her as one of them.

"I know they don't *have* to invite me home for dinner just because our pastors talked about hospitality from the pulpit that morning." She chuckles. "I think of it as God's love poking them in the rib, saying, 'Remember last week you said you'd invite someone this Sunday—now invite!' When God reminds them, I don't feel bad about it."

I'm firmly convinced that no one should visit our church and leave without being invited to someone's home. That doesn't always happen, but when it does, it is often contagious.

A young man named Bob Bickle was transferred to Salem and arrived ahead of his wife, who remained in San Francisco to finish her nurse's training. Bob visited our church Sunday morning, and was invited to someone's home for dinner that day.

The next weekend he flew back to San Francisco, rented a trailer, and drove to Salem. Sunday evening he called the church to see if he could hire a couple of young men to help unload his furniture. The elder who took the call relayed the message to the congregation, and after the service six young people volunteered.

The following Sunday evening, Bob was at the service and stood to say, "I've never experienced anything like the response of you people—like those kids who helped unload, unpack, and put away everything in a few hours—and refused to be paid. Furthermore, the first time I came here, I was invited home for dinner."

That wasn't the end of it. Two weeks later Bob invited the family, who had first invited him, to a homecooked meal at his house. He called his mother for her meatloaf recipe, and his wife for help with the gravy . . . long distance!

When Isabel Bickle joined her husband in Salem, they asked our family, along with a single young woman, for dinner. During our conversation, they happened to mention that they were having some people, "including the Iversons," for an evening of snacks and fellowship, and wondered if we knew someone else who would like to be invited.

My wife and I exchanged glances. The Iversons had eight children, while the Bickles had none. That morning I had talked to a new couple who were visiting the church and were looking for friends. I happened to have their phone number and gave it to Bob. He called, and I heard him say, "Pastor Bubna told us you were new in town and are looking for friends. We'd like to have you over to our house after church this evening to meet some other people."

I gathered that the new couple was delighted to accept the invitation. After hanging up, Bob beamed. "This hospitality thing is really neat," he said. "You've got to work at staying a stranger in this place!"

This sort of thing may not be too common, but it happens, and our church today is known as a hospitable group. That implies that our strategy for developing hospitality is working, but let me also tell you what percentage of our people are actively participating—so that if you were to start a similar program, you would not feel like a total failure if everybody in your group wasn't pursuing hospitality regularly within six months.

At this writing, it has been about eight years since we took our first survey on hospitality in the church. It has been thirteen years since I came to Salem and started talking about friendship evangelism and eating with people. Today we have roughly ten percent of the church actively pursuing hospitality while others are in the process of learning. Ten percent is enough of a significant minority to make all the difference.

Our strategy remains the same and will continue. There will always be a need for teaching about hospitality, for practicing it, and for encouragement and training. New people join our group, and we who have been around awhile need a reminder.

Just recently I preached again a series of messages on hospitality in the New Testament church. That makes the fourth time in twelve years. Our friendship hours are a permanent and growing tool for cementing the bond of love within the fellowship. We are continuing today what began as our first structured opportunity for hospitality, a ladies' friendship luncheon and men's breakfast given four times each year. These are held away from the church facilities, at a local restaurant or banquet room. The speakers are always lay people, preferably from our own fellowship. At these occasions we are each encouraged to bring someone we've befriended outside the church.

Originally planned as a vehicle for friendship evangelism, these events now fit into the larger perspective of hospitality as phase three in our growth strategy. Phase one is learning to be hospitable with each other; phase two involves Christians beyond our local congregation; and phase three deals with the nonbelieving coworker, fellow student, neighbor, or casual acquaintance whom we are learning to accept in friendship.

We are finding out more and more why hospitality is not presented as an option, but as a command to Christians. There is nothing like it to confront you with your own lack of love for others. Jesus said other folks would know we were his followers because we loved one another so much. How do you think that love became visible in the early church? It is not enough to shake hands with (or maybe even hug) a few of your close friends and nod with a smile at some of the familiar faces each time you see each other at a prayer meeting or worship service. It is when "loving one another" gets down to the nitty-gritty business of inviting to your home someone with whom you have very little in common—or perhaps don't even approve of—that you have to face your real feelings

The custom of sharing meals at each other's houses must have dealt effectively with the pride and prejudice that was as prevalent in the first century as it is in our day. What Jew with any self-respect would ever think of eating with a barbarian? Or what slave would be invited to his master's table? Non-Christians who observed the believers saw the evidence of love. "Look how they love one another—they even *eat* together!"

6

What Are We Supposed to Be Doing, Anyway?

There's an old story about a farmer who one morning decided to plow the south forty acres. His tractor needed oil, so he started for the barn to get it, but on the way he noticed that the pigs hadn't been fed. Near the corncrib was a pile of sacks, reminding him that the potatoes were sprouting. But on his way to the potato pit, he passed the woodpile and remembered that the kitchen stove was burning low. While picking up wood, he saw that one of the chickens was ailing, so he dropped the wood to doctor the chicken . . . and so it went till the end of the day, and he still hadn't oiled the tractor or plowed the south field.

The church of Jesus Christ, since its beginning, has had a main purpose, but often it has been so obscured that if you ask a hundred Christians what they think the church is supposed to be doing, you may get a hundred different answers.

Like the farmer, we tend to stay busy with good things that need to be done. But unless we keep our primary purpose in mind, all our efforts will be frustrated in the end, and we'll be as unproductive as a farm with fields left unplowed.

The Bible reminds us of our main goal in various ways, over and over again. Jesus gave his disciples what we call the Great Commission just before he ascended to be with the Father in heaven. It was his statement of purpose for the church: "Go therefore and make disciples of all the nations" (Matt. 28:19a, NASB).

61

Unfortunately, as a church, we've tended to focus on the "go into all the nations" aspect of the command, and failed to see that the central part of our purpose is "to make disciples." The word disciple means someone who is in the process of learning, like an apprentice who follows his master. So a disciple is not a finished product, but someone who is continually learning. We say of someone who never seems to get through with his education, that he is a "professional student." Jesus was saying that his church would be made up of "professional learners"—disciples who would never get through increasing in their knowledge of Jesus Christ as long as they lived!

Paul put it this way: our goal is to "present every man complete in Christ" (Col. 1:28, NASB). He refers to maturity and wholeness, man at his full potential, as he was meant to be. Jesus was like that. The Roman governor Pontius Pilate examined him and then presented him to the Jews who demanded that he be crucified, with the words, "Behold the Man!" (John 19:5, NASB). Here was an authentic man as God intended him to be.

In 1975 our church sponsored a number of Cambodian refugees. Among them was a couple, Joe and Molyse Kong. They committed their lives to Jesus Christ as their Lord and Savior shortly after coming to Salem. Within a year, Molyse became seriously ill, and after months of increasing weakness, she underwent surgery. At one point her heart stopped, and she was placed on a machine. The doctors informed Joe that his wife probably did not have very long to live. Several of us gathered to pray for healing, and Joe quietly said, "God is too high for me to ask why. I must believe him." His voice was firm. "The pot does not ask the potter, 'Why did you make me this way?' I accept what is best for my wife and for myself. For if God takes her, she will soon be with him."

Standing by the still form of his wife, as she lay in the intensive care unit of the hospital, Joe prayed: "Lord Jesus, I give my wife to you. I commit her to your care, because she is your child, and I ask you to give me wisdom and courage and strength, that your name might be glorified."

After his prayer ended, Molyse slipped away into death. Later, in the memorial service, Joe asked to speak to the several hundred people who were there. Cambodian refugees, Joe's co-workers at the Department of Forestry, people from nearby schools who had worked with the refugees, businessmen, and classmates. Many were not believers.

"From the human point of view I am deeply hurt. It is a tragedy for me to lose the one I love. We had twelve wonderful years together." Joe paused; but when he spoke again, his voice rang with a new assurance. "When Jesus was in this world he said, 'I am the Good Shepherd, and I know how to care for every sheep in my flock.' Therefore, he is my owner and manager. I belong to him, and I am completely satisfied with his management of my life."

His listeners were deeply touched. Many spoke to me afterward; others wrote. Some had wondered about Christianity. Now they said, "It must be the real thing. How else could a man have peace in the midst of one of life's greatest tragedies?"

We who are teachers and preachers in the church need to be careful. Our job is not primarily to communicate information, but attitudes. It is relatively easy to teach Bible verses, the Ten Commandments, and the Sermon on the Mount, but if somehow we haven't communicated Christlikeness, we are falling short of the purposes of the church.

Larry Richards, in his recent studies of the home, has said that where real significant changes are taking place among the children, it isn't because of the regularity of Bible reading and family prayers, but because there are models of Christlikeness in the home. The same holds true for the church. The way to communicate Christlikeness is to reflect something of the character of Christ in our own lives, and that makes the job a lot more difficult.

The attitudes we are to develop as we mature, are the attitudes of Jesus Christ himself. He said, "Come to Me, all who are weary and heavy laden, and I will give you rest. Take My yoke upon you, and learn from Me, for I am gentle and humble in heart; and *you shall find rest for your souls*" (Matt. 11:28, 29, NASB).

The attitudes that will give us rest from our struggles and conflicts, and will communicate God's love, are gentleness and humility. The King James translation of the Bible calls it "meek and lowly." These are not exactly virtues I as a young man wanted to strive for. I thought more of developing the ability to assert myself in a competitive society. But Paul leaves little doubt about the essential Christian attitudes when he writes: "Walk in a manner worthy of the calling with which you have been called; with all humility and gentleness, with patience, showing forbearance to one another in love" (Eph. 4:1, 2).

"Meek and lowly" are probably not the words most often used to describe the organized church. Instead, it has often been accused of being rigid, unbending, fanatical, critical, and full of pride—"holier than thou." These attitudes separate people and build barriers between them.

The church becomes a place where we play a game. Sunday morning we put on our best smile and our church clothes, and everybody looks at all the other smiling faces and thinks, "Boy, I must be the only failure here. Everybody else is a super-saint, so I better act like one too." We develop rigid rules of "religious behavior" and judge ourselves and others by whether or not we observe them carefully.

We get in trouble because we measure ourselves against perfection while we should be measuring whether or not we are *in process* toward our goal of maturity. If you ask a very young person how old he is, he's usually proud to report, "I'm seven, going on eight!" He doesn't seem to be ashamed that he isn't fifty yet. But ask a Christian how he's coming along, and he may put on an apologetic smile and say, half-jokingly, "Oh, I'm not perfect yet."

I haven't learned to be perfectly loving or patient yet, and some days my failures are more obvious than others, but that doesn't mean I'm defeated. It means I'm growing and learning.

It's no secret that periods of stagnation happen to Christians at all stages of maturity. There's only one way to get moving again, and that's to admit why we're stuck. John wrote to first-century Christians who were as familiar with the problem as you and I are: "If we say that we have no sin, we are deceiving ourselves, and the truth is not in us. But if we confess our sins, He is faithful and righteous to forgive us our sins and cleanse us from all unrighteousness" (1 John 1:8, 9, NASB).

Our mistakes are no surprise to God, and shouldn't be to us either. The good news is that he forgives us and is ready to supply the means for me to do the thing I failed in. I can count on his presence and power, and step out in faith to do what I couldn't do on my own, to be patient where I just blew my top; or to be kind where once I was harsh and ugly. He makes it possible for me to say, "I can't, but he can, so I can!"

A young man whom I will call Tom had been a part of our fellowship for four years when he divorced his wife. After eight months of counseling he decided to drop the divorce proceedings, and one Sunday evening in our sharing service he stood up and told the congregation:

"I decided to take life into my own hands and see if I could get along without God's help too much. Needless to say, I blew it, and for that I apologize to you. Now my wife and I are back together again, and going to counseling. Things are not fantastic, but they are a lot better than they were. Thank you for praying for us."

It took courage for Tom to say that, but it also showed that he was growing. How do you think we can learn that we aren't capable of doing things in our own strength? By trying and failing . . . over and over again. The more mature we get, the more dependent on Jesus Christ we will become. So we can expect to fail in our own strength as part of the learning process. In fact, we ought to be glad every time it happens! Remember, it is *his* qualities that should be increasing in us, not our own.

Perhaps it is hardest of all to recognize and encourage the process of growth in our own families. My three children know that their dad hasn't learned everything about patience yet. They tell me I'm improving a little, which says something about how things were before.

We parents try to teach our children the right things, and then we panic when they do something wrong. It is fortunate that God doesn't see us that way. Can you imagine him looking in exasperation at my umpteenth mistake and saying: "You're hopeless! I've told you a thousand times if I've told you once, and here you go doing your own thing again. I guess I could have saved my breath!"

Have you ever said something like that to your teen-ager? I'm afraid I have. Expecting instant perfection of our children brings frustrating deadlock in our family relationships; while seeing them as people in process frees us to appreciate and enjoy our children. When they no longer sense the pressure to live up to some impossible standard, they in turn relax, become more self-assured (because they know we accept them as they are), and often perform better—not because they feel they have to, but because they want to.

A family in which parents know they are in process, and can accept their children in process as well, is a loving and happy family. Communication lines are likely to be kept open across the generation gap as parents and children enjoy and encourage each other.

The church that knows it isn't perfect can be open and friendly. When Christians are accused of being serious and rigid, I think it is often because we are trying so hard to live up to the impossible standards we have set for ourselves. What a relief to be able to accept myself as I am—to relax a little.

Over the last years we have sensed a gradual change in the atmosphere of our church in Salem. People talk more freely, and linger in hallways or meeting rooms. There is the sound of frequent laughter—not irreverence, but shared joy; gratitude because God loves us as we are and we are learning to love ourselves and each other.

One morning in Sunday school class, a missionary on furlough shared that she had gone through a difficult emotional struggle the year before. Next to her sat a visitor who impulsively said, "Gosh, I didn't know missionaries went through things like that. I thought they had it all together."

The missionary laughed. "Last year was a brand new experience for me. I really learned something about how great God is when I need him most."

The church who keeps in mind the goal of producing maturing Christians will welcome the skeptics and the seekers. We can say to them, "It is OK to struggle with doubts or grope your way toward faith. It is even OK if you aren't sure you want to be a Christian yet. We're just glad you're here, and your presence makes our fellowship richer."

One of my good friends in Salem is a young caseworker and counselor named Dick Simpson. We met at the YMCA six years ago when my son Jeff and I were taking part in a program there. Dick knew I was a pastor when he asked me to play the role of an uptight, narrowminded religious father for a Human Relations Seminar for the Salem Police Department. I accepted, and Dick thought I did a great job. We decided to meet for breakfast one morning, and that was the beginning of a friendship that eventually brought Dick as a cautious observer to our Sunday morning worship service.

"I can only take small doses of your preaching," he told me in his forthright way, "but I really appreciate your friendship, and I like the warm relationships in your group."

He was an infrequent visitor. Months could pass between the times he darkened the door of our building. But we met for breakfast once in a while, and he accepted my invitation to a couple of men's fellowship breakfasts. By now I knew that Dick was a bright and very sensitive fellow who had been turned off by church groups during his teens, and found it difficult to believe there was a loving God who personally cared for him.

"But I'm intrigued by what I see in your fellowship," he told me. "I've never felt so accepted by a group of people before. I find myself wanting to be a part of it, and I sense that the people genuinely appreciate what I can contribute as well."

After four years, Dick began to attend the Sunday morning services regularly.

"No one tells me I have to be there, but I miss you people when I'm not there, and I get the impression you miss me." He smiled. "You know, with my sensitive ego I don't like to be always on the receiving end, but I really believe you people think I'm a person of worth."

"Even to God?"

His warm grin was Dick's way of avoiding my question. "I know what you're getting at," he chuckled. "But I'm not ready for that. Till I get there, it helps me to know that I'm appreciated by somebody."

"I hope you don't feel I'm putting you on the spot."

Dick relaxed in one of our living room chairs, sipping the coffee Dee had brought him. "You're not putting me on the spot, Don," he assured me. "That's what keeps me hanging around. No one in that church has cornered me to say I need to hurry up and get saved, but all I have to do is look at your faces. They tell me you have confidence in your God, and slowly I'm learning to have confidence in him too."

He laughed and looked at me sideways. "You people are like Cadillac salesmen. You're saying, 'Look, we've got the best in town. When you want it, come get it. We're not going to push it on you.'"

So what are we supposed to be doing anyway, as a church? We are to be growing toward maturity in Christ, glorifying God by letting his attitudes increase in us—and thereby making him known to a world who is seeking.

That is our primary purpose—all else flows from that.

7
Talking Together

As a young man I knew two older pastors who were both fine preachers, but neither would speak to the other because they always got in an argument. That didn't seem strange to me then, because I thought that as long as you believed the right things, it was OK not to speak with Christians who didn't agree with you.

Now that I am aware that spirituality affects our relationships, it concerns me a great deal when Christians don't talk together. One of the first signs of being filled with the Holy Spirit, said Paul, is that we speak to one another (Eph. 5:19).

There are more and more people in this world, but we seem to know one another less and less on a personal basis. The printing press spreads the written word, electronic devices transmit our voices and images and conduct our business. It is all in the name of progress, and may have increased our speed and efficiency, but an important thing is missing . . . the personal touch.

Last year I corresponded with a computer in New England about a magazine subscription. They sent me two copies of the first issue, but when I wrote them, no more copies came for months. Trying to straighten out the computer was a frustrating experience, but the worst part was the feeling that nobody back there really cared about me.

In the true church, a *personal* relationship exists between us, God, and other Christians. It means that someone cares deeply for us and we care for them. Yet the organized church is often seen as impersonal and cold by those who come to our building looking for acceptance and understanding.

A couple who recently moved from Salem joined a large church in an eastern city. They attended services every Sunday for six months, and hardly anyone spoke to them. The church offered excellent preaching and a fine Sunday school, but my friends felt a need for deeper fellowship. Finally they took the initiative to invite two other couples from the church to a football game and home for a snack afterward. From that point their new friendship developed into a small group that met for Bible study and sharing, but it was the newcomers to the church who had to take the risk of breaking the ice.

No matter how fine the preaching or how top-notch the activities program, no church can claim to be spiritual if the people don't talk together. I don't mean just talking to your friends or your own group, but also including the stranger. The goal of the church is to grow together into Christlikeness. To grow together, we must get to know each other, and getting to know one another involves talking together.

Are you a talking church? Or do you sit in the pew Sunday after Sunday with people you hardly know anything about?

Why is it so difficult for most of us to talk to someone we don't already know? Or even to say "hello" to a new person? Although I think I am a people-person, I've always felt a little uptight about meeting someone new.

Left to ourselves, we would probably stay in our safe little cliques, but the Bible is very specific in commanding us to speak and to greet one another affectionately. It even urges us to "greet one another with a holy kiss" (Rom. 16:16). Our greeting should go beyond the casual, surface exchange of polite nods and phrases. If we Christians are to be recognized by our love for one another, we must begin by greeting each other warmly.

Most of us find it hard to greet people we don't know. We feel embarrassed and awkward, fearful that they won't like us. Most of us are also certain that no one else feels the way we do. The first step in overcoming our timidity is to realize that we aren't alone. Everybody else would identify with us if we just let them know where we are.

To get the members talking, our church took a survey of our greeting habits and shared the findings in a service. We asked everyone, including children, youths, and adults to participate, but no one was required to sign the sheet. The questions were as follows:

1. When I see someone at church I do not know, I want to speak, but often feel hesitant because (check *all* that apply):
   a. it is hard to talk to new people
   b. I am not always sure they are really new people
   c. I feel they may not really want me to speak
   d. I don't know what to say
   e. sometimes I just plain feel frightened or embarrassed
   f. I always find it very natural and easy to speak to strangers, so none of the above really apply

2. When I see a stranger and a friend standing in the foyer (check *all* that apply):
   a. I find it easiest to speak to the friend
   b. I sometimes speak to the friend and not the stranger
   c. I generally speak to the stranger first
   d. I usually try to introduce the new person to someone else

3. How many people did you speak to (greet) this morning whom you do not know? (Check one.)
   a. none
   b. one or two
   c. quite a few
   d. most that I saw

4. I try to invite visitors—new people in our church—for dessert or a meal (check the *one* that fits best):
   a. frequently (2 or 3 times a month)
   b. regularly (about once a month)
   c. occasionally (5-10 times a year)
   d. rarely (4 or less a year)
   e. almost never

More than 90 percent of the people checked that they found it hard to talk to strangers. The reasons were the same for most of us: we are afraid people may not want to talk to us, and we don't know what to say.

We tend to see others as more important than we are, and so we are afraid to approach them. It is hard to believe that they feel the same way about us. "That's ridiculous," we say. "I know I'm just a nobody. How could they be scared of greeting *me*?"

There is a kind of game we all play to hide our feelings of inferiority from each other. In a church setting it may go like this: mrs. lowly sees MRS. BIG after the service and hurries out the side door to avoid greeting her. Not because she doesn't like her, but because she is thinking, "There is that attractive MRS. BIG. She has such grace and ability that she wouldn't want to talk to someone like me. I just won't embarrass her by saying 'hello.' "

Meanwhile MRS. BIG, who knows herself as mrs. little, sees the other woman slip away and is offended. She thinks, "I guess that clever MRS. LARGE is too important to speak to me."

If those two women could read each other's thoughts, they would hopefully laugh together over their mutual misunderstanding, and then set about getting to know each other without a mask.

Even in families, we can hold on to false images of each other. Once when I was thirty-six years old I visited my younger brother Paul in Minneapolis. During our growing-up years we had considered ourselves friends, but not as close as brothers can be. We were talking alone after supper when Paul said, "You know, Don, we were raised in different families."

"What do you mean?" I was puzzled.

"Well, your family didn't have an older brother, and mine did."

It had never before occurred to me how different our childhoods must have been. I listened in silence while Paul went on:

"You had great abilities in leadership, and when I came to college two years behind you, you were a class officer and student body officer and listed in *Who's Who in American Colleges*—I felt I could never live up to that."

"But that's ridiculous," I said. "You always had better grades than I, and besides, it always bothered me that my kid brother was a better athlete than I was."

We talked past midnight, an unusual thing for us, and both felt the liberating effect of our new honesty. We had never been able to talk about how each felt threatened by the other, and so we had always been in competition to prove that neither of us was as inferior as he felt.

That evening we found a new closeness and could laugh at having seen each other as a threatening MR. BIG.

Learning to take the risk of speaking to strangers is a process, and we are ready to begin when we know our common starting point. Most people learn best when they have the opportunity to hear it, see it, and then practice it. Our strategy in Salem worked right in with the pattern we were already using in teaching hospitality. We taught it, practiced it ourselves, and provided opportunities for doing it.

I make it a point to always try speaking to a stranger before greeting a friend in any gathering of the church. In classes or in the services, we often use an on-the-spot exercise we call the neighbor-nudge. It consists of teaming up with someone else to talk for two minutes on an assigned subject. We usually ask everyone to turn around and talk to someone directly behind them. The neighbor-nudge is a superficial structured experience, but it is a beginning. Barriers are broken down, making it easier to talk to one another after the service.

Our volunteer greeter corps offer more direct training in talking to strangers. Twelve couples are enlisted each month, and are stationed at each door after the service. Their task is to greet every person who comes through their door. The first Sunday of their assignment, they are asked to come thirty minutes early for a training session where we roleplay the greeting. Each greeter is handed a sheet with simple suggestions for greetings. It is meant as a springboard for further conversation, if you don't know what to say for a starter.

We first introduced our program during a regular service, and everyone in the congregation was handed a suggestion sheet. I discussed the main points from the pulpit:

Begin by introducing yourself. Then, if you are not sure
you know someone, try . . .
"Have we ever met before?" or
"I believe I've seen you here before, but I don't remember
your name . . ."
If in doubt ask, "Have you ever signed our visitor's book?"
Introduce the people to others nearby, by saying, "Have you
ever met _____?"

Next I invited someone from the audience to join me up
front, and I said, "The two of us are going to play like we're
coming out of church Sunday morning, and I'm going to greet
you."

We shook hands, and I said, "Hi, I'm Don Bubna, pastor of
this congregation, and I'm glad to see you here."

The other person, who happened to be someone I didn't
know, smiled and gave his name and said he was glad to meet me
too. From that point we talked easily. I found out that he was
new in town and welcomed him to Salem. We discovered a
mutual interest in a well-known football team, and in two minutes we already knew several things about each other.

Then I told the rest of the people: "Our fellowship as a church
is nurtured by our speaking to one another. Are you willing to
do that now? Would you stand up, turn around, and introduce
yourself to a person you haven't spoken to before? See if you can
speak to someone who doesn't want to be the first to say something. I'll give you just two minutes to try it."

I checked the clock, gave the signal, and after a slight hesita-
tion nearly everyone followed my example. The sound of buzz-
ing voices and laughter nearly lifted the roof! I had to speak
loudly into the microphone to remind everybody that the two
minutes were up.

"You can continue immediately after the service, or over a cup
of coffee later," I told the smiling, animated faces reluctantly
turning my way.

This common experience made us all feel closer, more like a
family. The exercises in greeting have a wider purpose than
teaching people what to say to each other. They provide oppor-

tunities for adults to step out of the nonspeaking habit and begin communicating with others.

One lively older woman who had been coming to our services for six months picked up her courage one Sunday to speak to a couple across the aisle.

"I introduced myself and welcomed them to our church," she told me. "But they told me they had been coming here for twenty years! So I said, 'Shame on you for not speaking to me first!' "

A church who is learning to greet one another warmly communicates the love of God to those who come to seek him. Mary Ellen Travis first visited us at the invitation of one of her high school students. She told me later:

"I came with mixed feelings and sat in the pew wondering, 'What am I here for on a Sunday morning when I should be home in bed?' Then the woman who sat down next to me turned to introduce herself even before the service began. She said, 'Hi, I'm Marilyn Graffenberger and we're glad to have you here.' I was dumbfounded. After the service three or four more came to introduce themselves. I had never been given such a warm welcome by any group of strangers before . . ."

Remembering someone's name when you have only met once takes a little effort, and I remember vividly one of my early disastrous attempts. It happened in the church at Pacific Beach. A man who had been to our service once came back to visit, and I felt awkward because I remembered his face and our earlier conversation, but not his name. So I resorted to an old trick, asking: "How do you spell your name; is it with 'e' or 'i'?"

The man looked at me a little strangely before answering, "With an 'i.' It's H-I-L-L."

Since I was the pastor, I couldn't slip away to hide my red face, but I've never used that method again.

Remembering someone's name shows him that you care. I have noticed that when I am more interested in what a person has to say than in what he thinks of me, his name sticks in my mind much easier. A few people have a natural talent for remembering everybody they meet. Most of us have to learn to remember. As Christians, I believe the Holy Spirit will help us, because recognizing someone by name is a way of showing love.

Today I try hard to really focus my attention on the individual I meet. If my mind is on something else while he mumbles his name, I am sure to forget it immediately. If it fits into our conversation, I usually repeat his name once or twice, and after our meeting I try to recall some of the main things he said, reinforcing my memory once more.

Educators have discovered that the greatest amount of unlearning takes place shortly after we learn something. It helps to repeat what you've heard as soon as possible. If you are teaching, the lesson should be reinforced with opportunities for practice right away. That's what we do in the Welcome Class which meets during the Sunday school hour between the first and second service. Originally planned for newcomers and visitors as a short introduction to basic Christian beliefs, the sessions were later expanded to a thirteen-week semester, repeated four times a year, and now are held as two six-month semesters yearly.

The Welcome Class has been called our "boot camp" in Christian relationships, and we start right off each Sunday morning by talking together. I put the first words of a sentence on the chalkboard, and we all take turns introducing ourselves by giving our name, occupation, and finishing the sentence. Those who want to are free to pass on the last part.

The sentences are usually related to our topic for the day. If we are going to talk about our individual worth in the eyes of God, I may write on the board, "One thing I like about myself is _____."

Other beginnings we have used are:
"The best measure of personal success is . . ."
"Today I feel . . ."
"I felt love when . . ."
"A friend is . . ."
"To get to know someone . . ."
"Other people usually . . ."
"When I have something to say . . ."
"I miss . . ."
"I sometimes think of people . . ."

"There are times when . . ."
"One of my pet peeves is . . ."
"I would like to be . . ."
"It's fun to . . ."
"Somebody who really helped me once was . . ."
Then I put a second optional question on the board, and this one is always the same from week to week:
"One thing I've been learning about the Christian walk this past week is _____."
The class has become a starting place for those who are hesitant about attending a formal church service. Ned and Joanne Kanoff came regularly to the Welcome Class for six months before going to the worship service.

"We couldn't handle the whole program at once," Ned explains. "But in the Welcome Class we were comfortable. There was no pressure. No one told us we ought to come to the service. We were encouraged and given the freedom to figure out what it was all about."

For Carole Meyers, the class was a "security blanket." "We met friends there that we're still very close to."

The warmth of real Christian relationships are often first experienced in small groups, and can then spill over into the larger fellowship. Old "graduates" of the Welcome Class often return to share with us. Not long ago, one said: "What I'm learning more and more is that the Christian walk isn't something you do alone . . . and it started for me in this room."

One of our elders, Tom Henkle, who is also a Welcome Class graduate, calls it "a key to the relationships in the church. Here newcomers immediately acquire a nucleus of friends. It often takes a long time to get to know someone in a new church. But here everyone gets an insight into each other through the question and answer session. No one sits in a corner, left out. Everyone has something to contribute."

We end our sessions with a reminder that it is important to express God's love to each other. Often we are told to communicate his love to the world, but that begins with our responsibility to one another. Then the world will take notice and say: "See how they love one another."

Before leaving the class, we are encouraged to speak to some-one we don't know very well, telling them we'd like to know them better. Or to thank someone for what he has said in class. Not only the world takes notice when we express God's love to one another; God hears and takes note too. Jesus said, "Where two or three have gathered in My name, there I am in their midst" (Matt. 18:20, NASB). God loves to join us whenever we get to-gether as Christians to talk. He wants to be in on our coffee breaks, our happenings, our sharing times; and he is listening to what we say. What an awesome thought. It has been estimated that the average person speaks about 30,000 words a day! When evening comes, most of us can think of a few words we wish we had never said.

The poet Carleton writes:

> *"Careful with fire," is good advice we know,*
> *"Careful with words," is ten times doubly so.*
> *Thoughts unexpressed may sometimes fall back dead,*
> *But God himself can't kill them when they're said.*

Who can control the human tongue? The answer to that is of course that only God can. The process of being changed into Christlikeness is first reflected in what we say.

Few things cheer up the atmosphere as much as saying nice things to each other. One of the neighbor-nudge exercises we use is to ask everyone in the room to say something kind about *someone else* to another person. We have done it at the end of a service and sensed the spirit of love and unity flood our meeting place.

Another tool of encouragement is what we call the encourage-ment card. A few years ago I visited a Baptist church in Houston, Texas, where they had stacks of small cards in each pew. They used them to write down prayers, and I thought the cards could be used to write notes of encouragement during the service. I brought the idea home and we printed up a bunch of cards with the verse from Hebrews about "encouraging one another." Usually after the sermon we take time to think of someone who needs a lift (and that is all of us) and write a few words of appre-ciation and love on the card. On the front we put the person's name (and if he is not from our fellowship, his address), and Tuesday morning our church office workers sort and mail the cards.

The encouragement cards have come to mean more to our people than I had ever thought they would. Our weekly volume of cards is increasing steadily, and in my drawer I have a file of them addressed to me. Each means something special. The children in the church are among our most eager writers, and the generation gap is closed when a first-grader writes to a senior citizen: "I heard you were sick. I love you and Jesus loves you."

During a sharing time, someone will always mention the cards. One mother said recently: "I want to thank all of you who wrote during our son's illness. We got 183 encouragement cards in two weeks!"

In addition to the card I write to someone during each service, I try to make it a part of my daily discipline to send a short note of appreciation, especially to those I work with. It takes less than sixty seconds to write: "Dear John: Thanks for what you did; it touched my life last Sunday." I can write several one-sentence notes in less time than it takes to make a phone call. And somehow a written thank-you means more than saying it next time we meet.

Learning to be an encourager is a long process. It means getting in the habit of thinking well of others and letting them know it. The cards are a tangible tool. Something we can go back and look at, again and again, and it cheers us every time. I visited an old church member in a nursing home shortly before she died. She had not been able to attend a service for several years, and could no longer speak. She gestured for her Bible, and when I handed it to her, she took out a treasured encouragement card. It consisted of just seven words saying that she was remembered and appreciated. And it brightened her life.

Active young housewives and mothers are in need of encouragement, too. A young believer says: "On a bad Wednesday morning I walk out to the mailbox and there is a card from someone who says, 'I love you!' Getting those cards makes me want to write more and more myself. It sort of snowballs."

Darlene Cue, a busy young mother, says: "Every service I

remember several people I want to write to. I've even tried bringing some cards home, but there is never time during the week. It is so good to be able to respond during the service when God brings someone to my mind."

One of our young men says: "I've sometimes wondered how many cards we would write if we didn't allow time for it in the service. I don't think there would be very many."

It isn't just a nice custom, we need it. We need to receive encouragement, and we need to give it. Expressing love to others not only builds them up, but also helps our self-esteem. As a church, our goal is to present every one of us mature and whole in Christ. None of us are finished products, we are in process, and that can sometimes be painful. It should also be exciting. Encouragement along the way not only helps us to get where we're going, but to enjoy where we are.

8
Come Cry with Me

Some years ago I was the speaker at a seminar for pastors in Canada. During one session several lay people were asked to tell us what they expect of their pastors. A veterinarian's wife in her thirties said:

"One thing I'd like my pastor to do is to communicate that he loves us. I know we need to be exhorted and corrected, but we also need to be told that we're loved."

One of the pastors asked her, "How do you want us to communicate this?"

"Simply by telling us."

"What do you mean?" He looked puzzled.

The lady surveyed the roomful of pastors and said, "Why don't you try standing in the pulpit one Sunday morning and say, 'I just want you people to know I love you.'"

It got strangely silent, while I felt ill at ease. I no longer believed, as I once had, that love was something mushy which only liberal churchmen talked about, while we evangelicals were properly concerned with true doctrine and theology. I had learned to say, "God loves you," but to say "*I* love you," and from the pulpit? Surely the people in my church already knew I cared deeply for them.

As a boy I had looked up to pastors as almost superhuman. When I became one and knew better, I still felt I ought to hide my emotions and weaknesses so that I would inspire confidence as a strong leader. Since I felt quite insecure as a brand new pastor, I started out by using the title "Reverend." It established my importance and set me apart from the rest of the congregation. Later, when I felt a little more secure, I called myself by the less exalted title of "Pastor." It took a lot longer to come to the point where I felt comfortable introducing myself simply as Don Bubna.

Like most males in our culture, I had been conditioned to hide my tears, while inside I always felt deeply with people who were hurting. We had been in Salem for nearly two years when I had to conduct three funerals in one week. The last was for a patriarch of the church whom I had deeply appreciated. My daughter Cindy, who was twelve, had said, "I wonder how Grandpa Gunther is doing, getting his new house straightened up in heaven." At the funeral I repeated her remark and was suddenly too choked up to go on talking for a while. It was embarrassing, because I had never broken down while speaking in public before.

Afterwards I confided in one of the men, "I really blew it today, didn't I?" He looked surprised and shook his head. "Pastor, we like to know that pastors are human too."

His words took me by surprise, and in reading my Bible it struck me for the first time that human emotions were portrayed quite openly there. Joseph was a grown man who held a prominent position in Egypt, but he unashamedly "wept a good while," hugging his father after they had been separated for many years. Neither did Jesus make an effort to hide his tears, and he was no sissy.

To openly say "I love you" from the pulpit seemed a risky thing to do, and I wondered if it was necessary. But the thought hounded me all the way home from Canada. "What if I haven't made it clear to the church that I love them?" I decided to make sure, and the following Sunday I stepped into the pulpit with more than the usual trepidation.

"I don't know if I have communicated this clearly enough," I said, "but I want to tell you this morning, I love you."

The place got so quiet I thought I had said the wrong thing. And then I saw some people wipe their eyes.

It was a new step for me, and the next came when I was able to say it straight to some of the people I feel close to. Years later a friend wrote:

> *Dear Don,*
>
> *I'm trying to evaluate the impact of your life on mine. One thing I know, and that means more than anything else to me: you really do love me. My brother, thank you—and I love you.*
>
> *Probably these words are extra hard for men to say to one another because of the cultural perversion of what love means. But maybe because it is harder to say, it means even more when it is said.*
>
>
>
> *Yours in him,*
> *Ross.*
>
>

Since it is our human tendency to pervert not only the word, but the emotion, I often talk about our need to be very proper with one another in the church. As a man I am not above having impure thoughts, and so I am very careful of the way I convey love for anyone of the opposite sex. I have found that I am most comfortable when I can say to a woman, "My wife and I love you and think of you warmly."

God does not dehumanize us when we become Christians. Emotions are dangerous when we allow ourselves to be ruled by them. Our behavior must be governed by the Word of God, not by how we happen to feel at the moment. But to deny our emotions is both inhuman and un-Christian. We should be no more ashamed of our tears than of our laughter.

The Bible instructs us to "Rejoice with those who rejoice, and weep with those who weep" (Rom. 12:15, NASB). A few years ago one of the young men in our church backed his tractor over his two-and-a-half-year-old son and killed him. It happened on a Saturday, and Dee and I went together to the home. On the way out, I remember thinking, "What do I say on an occasion like this?" I could think of nothing appropriate, but when we got there the wife threw her arms around Dee, and I embraced the man and said, "We've just come to weep with those that weep." And we did, and that seemed enough. Later there came the right time to talk about what had happened in the light of God's love and sovereign will.

Our love deepens when we share our sorrows and joys, and to hide these things from each other erects barriers between us. Fear, pride, insecurity, and shame separate us. To love one another, we have to show that we are human.

To a Christian, our humanness should convey two things. First, that we are created in God's image, so that each of us has great worth no matter what our individual differences may be. The second thing our humanness implies is that we share a common sinfulness. As a pastor I share the sinfulness of everyone else in the human race. To love one another means to accept both each other's worth and each other's imperfections.

To share on a deeper level requires honesty about our hurts and blemishes as well as the good things in our lives. That is never easy, but once we begin, we discover that others feel a great deal like we do. It becomes easier to keep our masks off the more we understand each other.

In the Welcome Class we have shared with each other, "One of my weaknesses is _____." As we take turns completing the sentence, we identify with each other, because there aren't any in our group without weaknesses.

Like Lon who repeats himself too much.

Or a grandmother who wants to help her grown children when they don't need help.

Or Pat who worries too much, Denise who is impatient, Tom who wastes time, Jim who is too loud, Marilyn who can't accept other people's weaknesses and is finding out that probably means she can't accept her own.

And John who watches too much TV, Debbie who eats too much chocolate candy, Al who loses his temper for no reason, Ann who has too many doubts, Kathy who is a procrastinator, or Linda who can't keep from meddling in other people's business.

Talking about it makes us feel closer. Deep friendships begin when we can say, "This is me and I'm not perfect."

Paul the Apostle must have looked pretty big and important to others. He made a point of telling his followers about his weaknesses and limitations, so that they would see his humanness and not feel threatened. He said, "Now I am glad to boast about how weak I am; I am glad to be a living demonstration of Christ's power, instead of showing off my own power and abilities" (2 Cor. 12:9, TLB).

The power of Christ is hidden when we look as if we've licked all our problems. We are saying, "Look at me, I'm a super-saint and God is lucky to have me on his side." Super-saints may be admired and even worshiped a little, but people sense that they are somehow unreal and are afraid to become their friend.

The pastors and other elders are responsible for setting the tone in the church. If we preach about Paul's honesty and urge the people to follow his example, but don't do it ourselves, we can't expect much result. In the eyes of the congregation, the pastor easily becomes a Mr. BIG who might be able to help them in their weaknesses, but who doesn't need any help himself.

When I first came to Salem, I sought to establish lines of responsibility and communication in the administration of our fellowship. Patience was not one of my strong points, and if things weren't done when I thought they ought to be done, I sometimes stepped in to take care of it myself. This invariably resulted in some bruised feelings and friction between lay leaders and their new hotshot pastor from Southern California.

A few months after I arrived, something happened in my relationship with the chairman of our building committee, Jack Hancock. Planning was underway on a new Sunday school and office wing, and Jack, who was a successful local businessman, was coordinating the work very efficiently. One day when I knew he was busy elsewhere, I called the architect. It concerned a minor problem, so I didn't take time to bother Jack.

Early the next morning, he called my office. "Hello, Pastor, I hear you called the architect yesterday." There was an unmistakable edge to his voice.

"Yes, Jack, I did." I felt slightly apprehensive.

"That's all right, Pastor. If *you* want to run the building program, *you* call the architect, but if you want *me* to run the building program, *I'll* call the architect. Do you understand?"

I managed to answer calmly, "Yes, Jack, I do understand, and I want you to know that I really appreciate the way you run the building program."

That evening I poured out my feelings to Dee. She brought us both a cup of Sanka, and sat down on our worn living room sofa, facing me. Her voice was soft: "Has it occurred to you that Jack Hancock may see you as a man who likes to take full charge of a situation, and that he possibly interpreted your phone call to the architect as a lack of confidence in him?"

"That's ridiculous." I spoke defensively. "How could anyone not have confidence in Jack? He is super-efficient."

There was a hint of a smile in Dee's blue eyes. "How could anyone not have confidence in you?"

Her words came back to me often during the next few days as I found myself watching Jack Hancock and some of the other men more closely. Did they feel threatened by me? The idea was preposterous. I saw them all as capable men, both in their professions and in the church. In contrast, I was new and untested in Salem. I had more reason to feel threatened in my position than any of them. Of course, I had not openly admitted to a lack of self-confidence, since I was sure this would undermine their trust in me as a leader.

Not long after the phone call to the architect, Jack Hancock and I met early one morning to go over some plans. Before leaving home I had lost my temper with our five-year-old. Driving to town, I couldn't shake the memory of my son's face. I had been unreasonable, and was aware that my work had demanded too much of my time and energy lately.

It was completely unlike me to confide a personal problem to someone in the church, but that morning I blurted out to Jack, "I really feel bad about not finding more time to spend with my son."

Jack's expression changed. "I know how you feel." His eyes showed deep concern. "I'm having the same problem with my two boys."

For a moment I forgot that we had met to discuss business and that Jack was one of the fellows who sometimes threatened my authority as a leader in the church. Instead we were fathers with a common problem, and that made us feel suddenly closer.

Jack spoke first, with a new tone in his voice. "How about doing something together, like taking the boys fishing?"

"That sounds great!" We grinned at each other, and it was a lot easier to talk about the building program now that I knew Jack and I were both less than perfect fathers.

One Saturday morning not long after that, we took our boys fishing off the Mill Creek Bridge. We had a great time, and for me it was a turning point. Jack had become my friend, not because he was impressed with my super-abilities, but because he identified with my humanness.

Not long ago I saw the same thing happen in a national conference for church managers. We were discussing strictly business until one district superintendent said, "I have really felt inadequate in my post this year, and one reason is a sense of being a failure with my kids."

Later in the day a lay leader stood up to say, "I want to thank you for sharing what you did this morning. I've been running from the fellowship of the church because I felt I couldn't talk openly about my feelings of inferiority and failure as a parent."

The atmosphere of the entire meeting changed after that, and a feeling of closeness and love began to take place. It was *koinonia*, and it happened because two men took the risk of removing their super-saint masks and admitting their needs.

There is a risk in exposing your humanness, and my lack of self-esteem had made me think that Jack Hancock and the other men I worked with would not accept my imperfections. I had feared misunderstanding and rejection, and because Christians are imperfect, there is always a chance of that. It doesn't happen often, if we are careful not to share the wrong things with the wrong person. Nor should we glory in hanging out dirty linen, which is a form of exhibitionism, and not honesty about where we are and what our real needs are.

When I know that others accept me with my imperfections, it is easier to believe that I am accepted by God, and I am able to accept myself better.

Unconditional love sets us free to be ourselves without fake fronts. Greg Edwards puts it this way: "I've gone down the hall in church and someone says, 'How are you today,' and I'm free to say, 'Not very well.' The person just smiles and says, 'Thanks for being honest and letting me know what you're going through.'"

It's great to be free to have a bad day, because that means I am free to fail without thinking I have blown the whole show. Since we are imperfect, our failures should not surprise us any more than they surprise God. He, in fact, expects us to fail, and it was because of our fouling things up that he sent Jesus Christ to set them straight again.

Not long ago I forgot to announce the Women's Tea during our missions week. That kind of oversight can be pretty disastrous, but I'm learning not to get too hung up when I commit irrevocable sins like that. The next time I appeared in the pulpit (the day after the Women's Tea), I was able to say, "I want you to know that God expects me to fail, so when I forgot to announce the tea, I was only doing my thing!"

It is always easier to talk about our successes than our failures. The temptation is always there, when I am asked to speak away from Salem, to tell about our fantastically successful programs. That would take some exaggeration and omitting of painful aspects of the truth. Aside from boosting my own ego, such boasting would cause my listeners to feel worse about their own struggles, and keep us from having an honest, helpful exchange of ideas.

In our humanness, it is easier for us to feel close to someone who is honest about his setbacks than with someone who's just been promoted ahead of us. It is easier for me to feel close to a pastor whose church is just a little smaller than mine, than to the man whose congregation is growing faster than ours and just passing us!

That's the way we are. It takes Christian maturity to be honestly happy when someone else wins the trophy we worked hard for. That's the kind of maturity we're to help one another grow toward. (Not the kind we are expected to have attained!)

We help each other more when we can be honest about our

blemishes than when we talk only about our triumphs. Val Barnes was PE teacher and head coach at a local high school. He was a hard-driving man, and as football coach he had something of a hero image. It was a surprise to us when Val resigned as coach, finishing out the school year as PE teacher, and then taking a job as assistant coach at another school in town.

One Sunday evening Val stood up to share with us that he and his family had been going through a crisis.

"I think you need to know a little about why I resigned as head coach and took a job as assistant," he began. "Some of the people who worked under me thought I was too hard. They got together, and I was forced to step down." He struggled to keep on talking. "It's been real hard for me and for my family. Losing what I've worked for has given me something of a failure complex." His voice shook. "My coworkers were mostly right. I wasn't tuned into their needs like I should have been. This whole thing has made me think more about who I am and what my relationship is to God and everybody else."

The old self-assured Val Barnes would never have let anyone see that he was hurting, and that evening he experienced something new for him.

"People responded with a depth of sincerity I had never seen before," he told me. "Men put their arms around me and I felt their love. I guess my big ego had turned them away before."

Val Barnes shares actively in the relationships of the church today. Men feel free to talk to him about their own struggles.

"I could never admit that I had problems before," he says. "Now I'm learning to rely on others and I need their encouragement as I struggle to be a better Christian husband, father, and friend. My own failures make me less critical of others. I can accept them for what they are and not expect them to be something else. I'm even happy in my job. I could never have been that before, learning to take orders after I've been the boss. I can accept it because I know that God has a plan, and what I called a misfortune has turned out to be a blessing."

Mutual sharing leads to mutual caring. Paul wrote to the Corinthians: "What a wonderful God we have . . . the one who so wonderfully comforts us and strengthens us in our hardships and trials. . . . So that when others are troubled, needing our sympathy and encouragement, we can pass on to them this same help and comfort God has given us" (2 Cor. 1:3, 4, TLB).

When we've been through some struggles and hardships and know what it is like to be comforted, we can begin to help others who go through trials. We can say like Paul: "I'm finding answers in my trials from God, and I want to share these answers with you where you are in your trials."

This kind of sharing is increasingly going on whenever our people get together individually or in groups. Sunday night services generally include a sharing session at the end when we are encouraged to let others know both our joys and our needs. Two people are ready with microphones, one on the lower level and one in the balcony. When someone stands to indicate he wants to share, the microphone is brought to him. When he has spoken, the pastor who leads the service gives an open invitation to anyone who especially identifies to respond with a word of encouragement or lead the congregation in prayer for the specific need.

A teen-age boy in our church got into trouble with the police and the story got in the newspapers. The following Sunday evening the boy stood up to say: "Some of you are aware of the difficulty I've been in with the police. I just want you to know I've made it right with God, but I want to ask your forgiveness because I've brought harm to the body of Christ."

Another young man responded: "I want you to know we forgive you." He sat down and Henry Turnidge, one of our elder members, beckoned for the microphone. He directed his remarks to the boy: "I want you to know that when I was a young pastor, I lied to the head of our elders. I told God I was sorry, and he told me to tell the elder as well. I didn't want to, because I thought the board would fire me; but I told him, and he forgave me. It took courage for you to stand up tonight and confess to us. I want you to know we appreciate it."

As he sat down, we all felt that the exchange of confessions had brought us closer together as a family.

Confessing to God is always easier than confessing to men, but James wrote, "Admit your faults to one another and pray for each other so that you may be healed" (Jas. 5:16, TLB).

The principle of confession must be used with wisdom. In many cases a public confession can do more harm than good. But when a barrier has been erected over some wrong which was done, we must put ourselves right both with God and with those who have been hurt.

Specialists in psychosomatic medicine tell us that a host of physical diseases are caused by unconfessed envy, jealousy, self-centeredness, resentment, fear, unforgiveness, and hatred. Dr. Hobart Mowrer, past president of the American Association of Psychologists, says that the early church had the secret for preventing mental illness—the confessing fellowship. The church today has largely lost that, and the world is finding it in small group therapy.

Not all our suffering and sickness is because of unconfessed sin, but often it is. A right relationship with God and others is a prerequisite for health and wholeness.

Carole Meyers says, "I used to feel guilty when I was so down and depressed that I couldn't even pray or talk to God. Now I'm beginning to think God planned it that way, because it makes me go to someone else and tell him or her where I hurt so that that person can pray *for* me. If I was always able to take my problems to God alone, I wouldn't need the church.

"The other day I had a problem and I felt so bad about it I couldn't pray. I told a friend who prayed for me, and the problem went away. Then I called her to tell her, and she said, 'You just made my day.' We shared not only the problem, but the answer, and that is what it means to belong to one another."

It is not a sign of spiritual maturity to make it on our own. We are learning that our love grows deeper as we come to depend not only on God, but on each other.

James wrote, "Is anyone sick? He should call for the elders of the church and they should pray over him and pour a little oil upon him, calling on the Lord to heal him" (Jas. 5:14, TLB).

Why must the sick one call for the elders? Why can't they just come to him if they know he has a need? I think it is because the confession of our need is an important step toward healing.

One of our elders went through a serious financial crisis several years ago. He became so depressed that his wife feared for his emotional well-being. I suggested he ought to call for the elders and ask them to pray for him. That was a hard thing for this man to do; he had always been strong before. But he did, and those men who loved him gathered around to place their hands on him while he shared his heartache and his fears. Within a short time, the sick brother was well, and the experience had deepened his compassion for others who suffered as he had.

A young woman who came to me for counseling kept herself aloof from others whenever she suffered attacks of deep depression. The people mistook her aloofness for snobbishness, and I suggested that she ought to tell them why she sometimes acted that way. One evening in the sharing service she stood up and said: "I want to tell you people that I need you, and when I don't talk to you sometimes, it is because I have such terrible depressions. I'm hurting and having such a hard time accepting myself."

As soon as the service was over, an elder who had suffered depression went to her and said, "Luanne, I want you to know I have gone through what you are going through, and I admire you for saying this tonight." It was a significant step for this man, and later he was able to stand up during a service and share his suffering publicly.

Unless we let others know our need, they don't know how to help us. One of our elders shared what he and other elders had often discussed: "We feel we don't do enough to help those who need it, but we can't do anything unless we know what the need is. We can't just run out and say, 'I'm ready to help now.'"

Jesus asked a man who had been a cripple for thirty-eight years, "Would you like to get well?" (John 5:6, TLB). Expressing our desire to be made whole is our first step of faith toward a God we believe can heal us. Confessing our need to others shows our confidence in their love for us. It is acknowledging our mutual relationship of openness, acceptance, and trust.

A lady in our fellowship who had deep physical as well as emotional needs came for counseling, and I told her, "Maybe you need to ask our elders to pray with you."

"I couldn't do that," she looked horrified. "I'd have to tell them what is wrong."

"That may be part of the healing process," I suggested. "Why don't you think about it."

A few days later she phoned. "I've decided to talk to the elders. Will you call them for me?"

"I understand the Bible to say that *you're* supposed to call the elders. That's an expression of your faith."

So she called the chairman of the elders, and as it happened, he wasn't home, so she told his wife all about it. The wife listened, then said, "Perhaps you had better call the vice chairman." The lady did, and got to confess her need twice even before she met with the elders. Later she told me that the sharing had been a meaningful and freeing experience for her.

We can't assume that people know automatically how we hurt unless we tell them. A young couple left our fellowship to go to the mission field. Two years later, the wife gave birth to a daughter in Africa. The baby was fifteen days old when she caught a virus and died within hours. Richard and Donna Faith immediately called their parents in Canada to tell them, and then called us. They flew straight to Salem to spend a few days with the church before going to Canada on furlough. The people had been told what happened, but when Richard and Donna came to the Sunday morning service, even their best friends of two years ago seemed awkward in greeting them and quickly left the young couple alone.

Richard and Donna, who had first come to Salem because they felt the people here would be sensitive to their need, were bewildered and hurt by the lack of response.

"We asked ourselves, 'What's wrong?'" Richard said. "Then we remembered the look on some people's faces and realized that they were silent because they didn't know what to say and were afraid to intrude in case we wanted to be left alone. We needed to let them know that it was all right to talk about the baby, and that we needed to share what had happened."

That evening, during the service, Richard and Donna chose to sit near the front in a side pew where they could see the faces of their old friends and be seen as well.

"At first they looked away, and I waited till I could catch their eyes and smile to show them it was OK," Richard said. "They looked startled at first, then relieved, and things were the way they had been between us before."

When the sharing part of the service began, Richard came to the microphone and said: "Donna and I are here because you are our family, and we need to share with you what has happened. We are hurting, but we want you to know that we understand this is something God intends to bless us through." He paused, and we who ached with him also felt the strength of his assurance.

"When Donna first became pregnant, we decided that if it was a girl, we would call her Julisia," Richard continued. "The name derives from a Zulu word, *i ju julisi*, which means 'causes us to go deeper.' Her short stay with us certainly is causing us to come deeper into the love and knowledge of God. So I want you to know that with the hurt, there is also a deeper awareness of God's love."

Looking over the filled pews, he concluded, "We are here because we know that God's love for us is part of our love for you and your love for us. To come here is a healing, strengthening thing, and we need that before going back to our work in Africa."

The barriers Richard and Donna had felt earlier in the day were swept away. Their openness allowed us all to experience the oneness of belonging to one another and to God. That evening we shared both tears of sorrow and of joy.

Before leaving Salem, Richard and Donna told me, "The love we felt here two years ago has grown deeper. We are encouraged and strengthened in our faith that God brought this into our life because he loves us."

"There are many here who are grateful you came," I told them. "Your Julisia has caused many to go deeper."

9
The Team That Has a Place for You

Not long after I came to Salem, a lady in the church called me. "I think my neighbor is ready to become a Christian," she said. "Would you go call on her?"

"Wait a minute," I interjected. "Haven't you already established a friendship with your neighbor and shared your faith with her?"

"Well, yes." She hesitated. "But I couldn't lead her to Christ; *you're* the minister."

I was happy to go see the neighbor, but the woman who had called me also needed to discover that she is as much a minister in the church as I am. It is a common misconception to regard the pastor as some kind of "professional" Christian who alone is qualified to minister to all the rest of the church.

That is not the way the early Christians started out. Peter wrote: "You have been chosen by God himself—you are priests of the King" (1 Pet. 2:9, TLB). If you are a child of God by faith in Jesus Christ, *you* are a priest, and just as significant in the church as the man who speaks from the pulpit.

When someone tells me he is all for *my* ministry, I say, "Wait a minute. I'm a minister, but so are you, and my job is to equip you for yours."

The Latin word for *priest* means "bridge-builder." God has made us the bridge-builders from people to himself. Through our lives they come to know him.

There is a story about a somewhat mentally retarded boy whose name was Joey. He was in a singing group, but sometimes he presented such a discipline problem that the director thought of dismissing him from the group. Then one day he met Joey's father, who told him, "You know my boy isn't as smart as most people, but he is responsible for leading his mother and me, his grandparents, five brothers, and a sister to a relationship with Jesus Christ."

The director no longer thought of dismissing Joey. What a priest, what a bridge-builder!

Each of us has been given unique abilities by the Holy Spirit, and they are needed to keep the body of believers functioning, just as the different members of our physical bodies are needed to keep us going. My heart contributes to the rest of my body, and so do my lungs and my legs. Their special abilities would not mean much to them if they refused to be a part of the rest of me. Nor could I get along very long without them! The same kind of interdependence becomes very obvious when we take a look at the gifts listed in the New Testament.

I know of no two Christians who function alike, even with the same gift. Two widows in our church both are uniquely gifted to help others. Bertha Friesen is quiet, but with a cheerful smile that says more than many words. She and her late husband for years served delicious church dinners, and Bertha must have washed thousands of dishes and poured as many cups of punch. Now that her husband is gone, Bertha has taken a blind woman into her home to care for her. She is uniquely gifted to do what she is doing in a way no one else could.

Verna Sturdivant is a retired schoolteacher in her seventies. She is afflicted with Parkinson's disease, and first volunteered to answer the phone in the church office. That is when I discovered that Verna is one of the most direct and outspoken individuals I know. This sometimes caused her to be a little abrupt on the phone, but also revealed a special ability to cut through all small talk to the heart of an issue.

I asked Verna to put in order and catalogue my personal library and papers, and she came up with a remarkably efficient system. She now spends several hours every week filing, cataloguing, and keeping my office in order. Another of her unique abilities is doing research for my sermons. We meet weekly to discuss my topic, and she digs out background material and illustrations from the libraries in town.

No one could do what Verna is doing in quite the same way. She also takes young people into her home to live and do the chores that Verna, with her physical limitations, can't do. With sharp wit and candid ways, Verna communicates love in her own unique manner and touches the lives of people of all ages in the church. Verna and Bertha have the gift of serving others—yet certainly not in the same way. And we need them both as much as they need us.

During World War II I belonged to a boy scout troop that participated in Civil Defense activities. I volunteered to be a messenger who would assist the Air Raid Warden. I was thirteen, skinny, and small for my age, and I still remember the Assistant Scoutmaster saying, "Who could use a small kid like you?"

When you feel that you really aren't needed, it hurts. God has made us so that we have a need to feel that we are of worth and making a significant contribution. And God has so designed his church that when we say we need you, we aren't saying it just to be nice—it is true. Each gifted believer has a unique contribution to make, and we function best when we are all together, because our gifts are designed to balance one another.

The prophet/preacher is given the special ability to speak the truth of God to his generation. Like the Old Testament prophets, today's prophet/preachers can be a little abrupt and abrasive as they say, "Listen, you people, this is what God is saying to you!" If the gifts of preaching and administration weren't balanced by the gifts of encouragement and mercy, we'd be polished to nothing.

On our staff, Ted and I are most unlike each other. Ted, among other things, has the gift of mercy, of compassion and caring. I tend to be harsh at times, particularly in the area of administration. I know the church is glad we have Ted to balance me.

When some of the gifts are not functioning, the church appears sickly and ineffective. It still functions, just as my body learns to get along with a faulty heart valve or a broken leg. But it slows me down, and there are some things I can't do.

The purpose of our special gifts is twofold. One is to get the job God designed for his church done; the second is to get us "done" through doing it. Ted and I once defined the purpose of leadership as "getting things done through people the way they are best equipped to do it." Now we are learning that the purpose of Christian leadership is also to get people done—complete and mature in Christ—through their involvement in the ministry of the church.

John Carney, who once dropped out of Bible school in rebellion against what he called a negative and legalistic "churchianity," discovered the importance of the church in our fellowship. Today he is a very effective worker with our more than sixty junior high-school kids, and says:

"I've come to realize that God has put all his marbles in one basket called the church, and it is impossible to grow in my Christian life without being involved in some kind of ministry. I hear God saying to me, 'John, you really want to grow, you want your life to count for me? The only way it can happen is if you work through my church.'"

Your special abilities are given for the purpose of building up the church, but also for you to develop your full potential as a person. And that can only happen as you use your gift.

The special ability of pastor is only mentioned once in the New Testament. Paul wrote:

"And He gave some as apostles, and some as prophets, and some as evangelists, and some as pastors and teachers, for the equipping of the saints for the work of service, to the building up of the body of Christ; until we all attain to the unity of the faith, and of the knowledge of the Son of God, to a mature man, to the measure of the stature which belongs to the fulness of Christ" (Eph. 4:11-13, NASB).

The pastor/teacher appears to be a combination gift and he has the responsibility of equipping the rest of the people for their work. While the apostles, prophets, and evangelists often traveled from place to place to establish new churches and strengthen the ones that were already there, the pastor/teachers were settled with the local groups.

The word *pastor* comes from a word meaning shepherd, which means "the guardian and leader of a flock." As a teacher, he also feeds the people with knowledge and understanding. Unfortunately we've placed more emphasis on the teaching, lecturing role of the pastor, than on the leading part. The shepherd walks before his sheep; he doesn't drive them from behind. The pastor is to be a living example of the Christian truths he proclaims from the pulpit, so that the people will want to follow him.

It is quite all right to call a pastor a minister, but the term can be misleading, since we often tend to think of him as *the* minister. The ministry in the church is not from one to the many, but all of us serving one another.

To call the pastor "elder," is also correct, but equally misleading if we think of him as *the* elder. The word elder does not mean a special ability, but suggests maturity. The church is to be ruled by a number of elders, mature Christian men who may have different gifts, and one of whom is the pastor.

Elton Trueblood, in his book *Incendiary Fellowship*, suggests that the word which best describes the role of the pastor is "coach." Not that he should be called coach, but that this describes what he ought to be doing in the church—coaching the rest of the team.

In February 1973, *Time* magazine did a special writeup on John Wooden, UCLA basketball coach. They asked him, "What is your philosophy of coaching?" and he answered, "Get the players in the best of condition, teach them to execute the fundamentals quickly, and drill them to play as a team."

Some of the players were interviewed and said about their coach, "His ability to develop talent is unparalleled." "He molds five different personalities into one." "He's the kind of man you believe in and want to be like."

The good coach is more interested in developing his team than in scoring for himself. The good Christian pastor/coach should be more interested in developing others than in enhancing his own prestige. I should not want to make my church known as "Bubna's church," but as a living local body of Christ where Don Bubna is one of the maturing Christians. My special job in the fellowship is to equip the saints for their ministry, as the coach develops the players for his team. This ought to be the primary motive for everything I do.

I am not the coach because I already know the answers. The special gift of "coaching" is also one that develops with use, so I continue to be a learner along with the other disciples in the church. I am a better equipper of the saints today because I learned how *not* to do some things in the past, and I will hopefully be equipped to do some things in the future that I am not getting done today.

A young woman who became an enthusiastic worker in our Junior High School department shared with us what she was learning:

"After I was married my mother once told me, 'I can't understand how you can be such a good housekeeper, because your room was a total mess the whole time you lived at home.' I told her, 'You see, now I realize I'm not just responsible to myself, but to my husband as well, and that has made a difference in my life.'

"In the Christian life it is like that. When I have junior high kids to teach, I am no longer living just for myself. They are looking at my life, and that causes me to come closer to God. It is a tremendous discipline. It firms you up, because you can't be a phony before the kids."

Pastors too often try to teach maturity from the pulpit, but that is only one aspect of the coaching role. In addition, we need to be personally involved with individuals, and sometimes tutor in specifics. Obviously a pastor can't spend that much time with each developing saint in his church, unless there are only a dozen members.

Jesus' strategy for church building was to pour his life into trustworthy people who in turn would pour their lives into a trustworthy few, who in turn would touch others with the love of God, and so it would spread and never lose the personal touch.

I think this is the most difficult thing for me to learn; that an important part of my time should be spent with a few people, not to the exclusion of others. That's a tricky balance. And how do you find the trustworthy few? The first church I pastored was in a beach area with many apartment buildings and transient people. We had a high turnover of members, and I kept wishing God would send us finished saints who could be true leaders of the church. That never happened, and I finally realized that Jesus had chosen twelve to begin with who would hardly have been my choice.

Since he is still the Lord of the church, he keeps calling those to leadership whom I have difficulty recognizing at first, and he expects me to grow with them as we develop into a team together.

All the elected leaders of the church are not always the people God has gifted for leadership, but from among them will usually emerge the significant few. To find them, I have for as many years as I have been a pastor invited the elected officers to meet with me for a weekly prayer time together. Only about half show up with any regularity, but those who come are the ones I believe God wants me to work with.

An average of twenty men now meet Tuesday mornings, and another dozen on Saturdays. Our format is flexible, but always includes evaluating what is currently happening in the church, sharing what we're learning from God's Word, and praying together. Afterward we go out for breakfast to a reasonably-priced eating place in town. The Saturday breakfast is always at the Memorial Hospital cafeteria and after eating, several of us go upstairs to see a few people who are sick. This too becomes a discipling experience.

We now have a paid staff of four pastors and from two to six interns who are students or graduates of theological schools, training for full-time Christian work. Most multiple staff relationships in churches are not happy ones, and tend to have frequent turnovers. Perhaps it is because we are inclined to follow the world's approach to management in seeking men with certain professional qualifications and hire them to perform "their thing." Jesus Christ sought first to develop a personal relation-

101

ship with a man, then developed his abilities in a discipling relationship.

Mature Christian leadership is something that develops over many years of working and growing together. It must be based on a firm commitment to one another as Christian brothers and sisters, and the commitment invariably has to be tested through some difficult times. This has to be so, because our relationship as a staff becomes the model for the congregation. They should be able to see us work out our interpersonal relationships in terms of the love and faith we proclaim. Paul and Peter and Silas and Barnabas obviously had their strong differences of opinion, and we read that they clashed on numerous occasions. Yet these men deeply loved one another, and their love was the more remarkable because they did not always agree.

I have frequently heard remarked in our church, "I can see that Christianity really works when people who are as different as our staff can work together with such love."

It isn't easy, and there are some touchy moments, but we each sense that this is something we really need. It is our primary calling as shepherds to live the example of God's love, and without it our teaching falls flat.

Discipling others becomes a highly individualized and personal thing. As a staff we meet twice a week for a working conference, and we try to get together informally as often as possible. Two or three times a year, we have a working retreat with our spouses, with family get-togethers in between.

Each of the four pastors tries to determine five or six people to pour his life especially into for a period of a year. These men in turn are encouraged to develop special discipling relationships with a few more each.

On a broader basis, our newly elected officers start the church year with an officers' orientation day, when we give written job descriptions and some very basic instructions on how to conduct committee meetings, make up an agenda, and give a report to the congregation or executive committee. We have found that most people are hesitant about taking on a responsibility in the church, not because they don't have time, but because they've never done anything like that before, and don't know how.

So we make our orientation very practical. The staff or experienced elders go along the first time someone goes to visit a family on a regular call. Often we roleplay an unfamiliar situation. A very helpful thing is to get together afterward to talk about how it worked. Jesus did that with his disciples. He sent them out two by two with specific instructions on how to act and what to say, then gathered them to talk about their experience.

Brad Coleman was a student in law school when he first came to our church. His first official responsibility in the fellowship was to be Assistant Sunday School Superintendent, and part of his job was to recruit, interview, and train workers for children. Brad had never done anything like that, so we roleplayed it. I first "interviewed" him, then he "interviewed" me. He was a senior at that time, and I was a little afraid that he would think we were being silly. After he had made his contact, he came back to talk about it, and I said, "What did you think?"

He grinned. "I graduate next year from law school, and I had been wondering how to interview clients when I get to be a lawyer. This is one of the most helpful things I've ever done!"

Brad has served as vice chairman of the Executive Committee, and more recently of our elders, which means he leads all the sessions of the ruling body of the church. He is only one of several men who have been with our fellowship for a relatively short time before emerging as one of the "trustworthy few" who welcomes the discipling process for leadership.

It is a process, that once started, multiplies as you go along. Darryl Cue, who is a teacher at the school for the deaf in Salem, had only been with us a few years when he was elected chairman of the Deacons. He said:

"We came here and saw all these people involved in the ministry. It is a tremendous thing. It puts the emphasis on the worth of each individual. We are learning that the Lord has given each of us special abilities to minister to one another and build up the church to show the love of Christ to the world."

Recently we hung a seven-foot chart in the hallway, listing several hundred official service opportunities within the church. In addition, there were almost as many temporary needs.

I've known a few people who have said, "I'm not sure what

my gift is, so I won't do anything." The tricky thing about special gifts is that we seldom know we have them until we use them. Most things in life work that way. You don't know you can swim till you get out there and do it, and you get better the more you practice it.

The Puritans said that if something was unpleasant, it had to be God's will. I don't find that idea anywhere in the Bible. Quite the contrary. The Greek word *charisma*, which means gift, comes from the root word *char*, which means joy. Your gift is not just to be a joy to others, but to you as well. Jesus said he found great joy in doing God's will.

If you want to discover your gift, think first of what you have a real desire to do. When new people come into our fellowship and seem reluctant to get involved, I suggest that someone visit with them and find out what they really enjoy doing. That is often the clue to their special ability in the church.

Once you've decided what you'd like to do, you need to try it. If your hunch was right, you'll soon see some evidence that you're on the right track. Although you may never have done anything in that area of service before, you'll catch on rapidly and improve right along. That's the proof that you're not just working in your own strength, but the Holy Spirit has gifted you. The special abilities God gives us are more than we can attain ourselves. We can probably be effective in many things, but we excel in the special area God has gifted us for.

That doesn't mean we automatically become full-fledged supermen and wonder-women. God has wisely made hard work a requirement for the development of our special abilities. But the gift must be there before it can be developed.

The second kind of evidence that we're functioning in the area where God has given us special abilities is recognition from others. We should be slow in announcing, "My gift is . . . ," but rather let others tell us first.

Edward Lear, the British humorist of the last century, fancied himself a great painter, but few others thought so. Instead, it was Lear's nonsense verse and limericks which he wrote to please children which won him fame and fortune.

Many Christians are like Lear. They think they are qualified in fields where they have little ability, and so they misdirect their efforts and waste their energies. They sing in the choir when they should be teaching Sunday school, or teach when they should be caring for babies in the nursery or serving on the landscaping committee.

We have a responsibility as a church to let people know when we are being helped by their special gift. Our recognition of their gift is not only an encouragement, but may help them see the purpose of God for their lives.

Several people who have worked actively in our church have come to sense that God wants them to expand their ministry into a full-time Christian vocation. It is never easy to make a decision to change the course of your life. That is why we ask those who feel God may be calling them in a new direction to share this with the congregation. They need to hear from the rest of us if we sense that they have shown special abilities in the area where they want to serve.

Dale and Mary Jo Bagley had worked effectively with our Junior High Department, when they felt a desire to go into full-time Christian work. Dale told the congregation:

"We would like to go back to school and prepare for a full-time Christian vocation, but where do you see us fit into the body of Christ? Have we ministered to you in such a way that you can see us doing this full-time?

"We value your opinion, because we don't want to get into something we're not equipped for. We would appreciate it if you would tell us whether you think we need another year or two in a secular job here in Salem, or even if you think this is where we belong and we shouldn't go on. Whatever you tell us, we will take it to be God's word to us at this crossroads."

There were many among us who felt that Dale and Mary Jo had shown abilities that indicated a full-time Christian vocation, and told them so. The young couple went on to school, and later returned to Salem as interns on our staff.

When someone from our local fellowship leaves to serve on the mission field—and that has happened regularly over the last seven years—we hold a commissioning service. An important part of the service is when the people of the church stand to share how the new missionaries have helped them in a special way. As a church, we can commend them for ministry overseas because of the evidence of their ministry in our lives.

The final evidence that you have found your unique place in the body of Christ is that people are helped in their relationship to God and each other, and this gives you a sense of joy and personal fulfillment nothing else can do.

Sarah Kliewer was past retirement age when she began working as a volunteer in our office. She had never done office work before, but soon she had devised a weekly visitation schedule for the staff, and a helpful file of "caring cards" recording visits and special information about people as they came into our fellowship. She also took it upon herself to keep an attendance record by sitting in the back of the sanctuary and looking at the people who came to the Sunday morning worship service. She knew them all by sight, even when our attendance climbed past five hundred. When someone missed a service, she thoughtfully mailed him a bulletin the following week. Today we have a team of "checkers," people with a special gift for remembering faces and names, who especially enjoy making everyone in our growing family feel welcome when we are here, and missed when we are absent.

Sarah Kliewer had invited some young missionary candidates home for tea, and was telling them of her work and how much she loved it, when one of the young people asked, "How old are you?" With a gracious smile Sarah answered, "Not nearly as old as I used to be!"

She knew the joy and personal fulfillment of helping others through using the special abilities God has given her.

10
The Greatest Need in the Church

What do we need most in the church? More love? Yes, of course. Not a vague something we talk about, but a practical happening. Whether two people or a thousand are involved, practical happenings don't take place with any regularity with out some give and take.

That brings us to the issue of authority and submission, per-haps the trickiest aspect of human relationships. It is also the one most misunderstood and misused down through history, even in the church. For love to become a practical reality—in our home, church, or society—we have to learn the proper relation-ships of authority and submission.

It was the rebellion of the first man, Adam, that brought imperfection in relationships, and God ordained that some would be leaders and others followers, or else we would have chaos. Proper use of authority and submission would insure individual fulfillment and freedom. Instead, we have seen how the strong have used leadership to lord it over the weak, in the church as well as in the world.

Jesus Christ was given authority to execute judgment over a fallen world. He used that authority to submit to judgment him-self in our place on the cross. God then established his church—with Jesus Christ as the Head—to demonstrate his love in action among humans. It was to be God's way to "show and tell" how human relationships were meant to function through the proper use of authority and submission.

That was to be the key to love in the church. Certain qualifications were listed for the selection of elders who would have authority to rule the fellowship, not according to the pattern of the world, but as Jesus had taught his disciples:

"You know that those who are recognized as rulers of the Gentiles lord it over them; and their great men exercise authority over them. But it is not so among you, but whoever wishes to become great among you shall be your servant; and whoever wishes to be first among you shall be slave of all. For even the Son of Man did not come to be served, but to serve, and to give His life a ransom for many" (Mark 10:42-45, NASB).

On the last night before he was arrested and taken to be crucified, Jesus and his disciples were gathered in an upper room in Jerusalem for the last supper. Some of the disciples got into an argument about who among them would be the greatest in God's Kingdom, and Jesus rose up from the table, took off his coat, and wrapped a towel around his waist. Without a word he began to wash road-dust from the disciples' feet. It was the job of the lowest servant, and Peter objected, but Jesus insisted. After he had finished and reclined with them at the table again, he said:

"Do you know what I have done to you? You call me Teacher, and Lord, and you are right; for so I am. If I then, the Lord and the Teacher, washed your feet, you also ought to wash one another's feet. For I gave you an example that you also should do as I did to you" (John 13:12-15, NASB).

I am sure the disciples were both puzzled and a little annoyed with the words and action of their Lord. They were dreaming of holding important positions in a new world order, and the prospect of washing dirty feet didn't appeal to their human egos.

As a boy I had great ambitions for my future, but there was one position I never aspired to: that of a servant. Servants had to do things no one else wanted to do, and as the oldest of three brothers, I had already learned to use my authority to claim the better household chores.

When I was a senior in high school, my parents decided that

our family would be the janitors for the new building our church had bought. We moved into a basement apartment, and guess who got to clean the four rest rooms twice a week?

You guessed right, but I didn't like it. When I first became a pastor, and sometimes quoted Jesus' words about being a servant, I thought my "servanthood" properly consisted of being the leader, while I urged others to serve by doing the "lesser chores" of singing in the choir, teaching Sunday school, or being on committees.

God chose to place imperfect humans as leaders in his church, and that hasn't changed since the first century. The imperfect leaders of today are still tempted to rule as the world rules, by demanding strict obedience from their subjects. The result is resentment and rigidity instead of an alive and loving fellowship.

Perhaps the difference between the world's pattern for authority and that of Christ can best be illustrated by the story of a woman who was married to a tyrant. He gave her a written list of duties and regulations, and exercised rigid control over her actions, but she never seemed to be able to do everything he asked of her.

The tyrant died, and the woman married a kind and loving man who selflessly gave of himself without demanding anything in return. Several years later the woman came across the old list her first husband had written. To her great surprise she realized that she was doing all the things that had once been required of her, but with joy.

It was only when I realized that my authoritative manner didn't produce enthusiastic response in my fellow workers, that I began to understand that it was Jesus' *attitude* of servanthood that made the difference.

Paul wrote: "Have this attitude in yourselves which was also in Christ Jesus. Do nothing from selfishness or empty conceit, but with humility of mind let each regard one another as more important than himself" (Phil. 2:5, 3, NASB).

Paul wasn't just writing to the people who were to follow the leaders. He was addressing *everybody* in the church, including the pastors and elders. Perhaps especially the leaders, because they were given the authority to rule the fellowship. It is easy to consider yourself more important when you're put up front, and that attitude destroys the principal task of leadership; that of building others up, encouraging them to grow, and being their example in Christlikeness.

Peter was quite specific on this point: "I exhort the elders among you . . . shepherd the flock of God among you . . . not under compulsion, but voluntarily, according to the will of God . . . nor yet as lording it over those allotted to your charge, but proving to be examples to the flock. . . . You younger men, likewise, be subject to your elders; and all of you, clothe yourselves with humility toward one another, for God is opposed to the proud, but gives grace to the humble" (1 Pet. 5:1-5, NASB).

Peter doesn't tell the elders to make sure the younger men submit, because true submission can only be a voluntary action. Most of us have a false concept of submission. We think that being put down makes us automatically submissive. That isn't true. The wife who is dominated by an oppressive husband isn't necessarily a submissive wife, although she may be doing everything she is told. She may be just suppressed and resenting it. Her resentment is felt by her husband who in turn tends to become more oppressive.

The Bible tells wives to submit to their husbands, even the harsh and demanding ones. Meaningful submission is an inner attitude of consideration for the other person that makes him feel worthy and loved. Such an attitude does not develop on demand from the husband. Instead, the Bible tells him to love his wife with the same selfless love that Christ has for his church, the love that caused him to give his life for us.

So in reality, both husband and wife are told to consider each other more important than themselves. They are told to practice mutual submission, or mutual servanthood.

The ability to submit requires a healthy self-image. Submission implies a willingness to bend my will to others, and consider them more important than I am. If I feel unworthy and insignificant, I tend to be defensive, aggressive, and boasting to cover my insecurity. My behavior becomes assertive, competitive, and threatening, the very opposite of submissive.

When my self-esteem is low, submission seems a fearful and

threatening thing to my already bruised ego. Only the Holy Spirit can give me the inner assurance of self-worth that makes me risk bending my will to someone else. That assurance grows as we are appreciated and encouraged in a *koinonia* fellowship of believers.

Submission is the mark of spirituality, and as we mature in Christlike qualities, we should become more submissive, more loving. That speaks to me of the fact that elders should be the leading examples of submission in any church.

Why all this talk of submission? Can't we be loving without it? Not really. Because to be truly loving means that I am willing to consider someone else's needs before my own. Another word for that is submission.

Submission is also the key to our relationship with God. The only way to find my new life in Christ, the new birth, and the fulfillment of my potential as a unique child of God is through the voluntary act of bending my will to the will of God. Another word for that is submission.

Ever since I was a child, I have known the verse, "If anyone wishes to come after Me, let him deny himself, and take up his cross, and follow Me. For whoever wishes to save his life shall lose it, but whoever loses his life for My sake and the gospel's shall save it" (Mark 8:34, 35, NASB). For many years these words of Christ made little sense to me. How could I find my life if I lost it? Or lose it if I found it? It was a mystery, and I used to think it only applied to Christian martyrs who died at the hands of their persecutors.

It was Judy Garland who finally brought it all into focus for me. I never met her, but we grew up at the same time; and while I was still playing sandlot football in St. Louis, she was a star who won an Oscar for her performance in "The Wizard of Oz." She was something of an idol to my group, who thought that if anybody had it made, it was Judy Garland. I lost track of what was happening in her life, until I came across an interview with her as she was getting ready to marry for the third or fourth time. She was quoted as saying, "I have finally found happiness." Two weeks later she committed suicide.

It made me sit down and consider some things about my own

life. As a teen-ager I had dreamed of winning fame and fortune, but instead I made the difficult decision to follow Christ. I thought I was giving up a lot of things, but instead I found more happiness than I ever thought possible. I wouldn't trade places with anyone, and sometimes I feel almost guilty for being paid a salary for doing what I enjoy the most.

We resist submission to God's will because we think it means an end to everything we've ever wanted. The death to self is never easy, but the end result is a new and better life. Before the foundation of the world, God ordained the principle of submission before exaltation. God's way up is down, even for himself, in the person of his Son, "Who, although He existed in the form of God, did not regard equality with God a thing to be grasped, but emptied Himself, taking the form of a bond-servant, and being made in the likeness of men. . . . He humbled Himself by becoming obedient to the point of death, even death on a cross" (Phil. 2:6-8, NASB).

Jesus could submit, even to the cross, because he knew his worth as God's Son. His submission was the key to our new life, but it requires our submission of the old life before we are free to live the new one.

Somebody says, "Man, that's really being a loser. That's a bad trip for life!" No, it is not, because remember, it doesn't *end* at the cross, at the point of submission. The new splendor *starts* there.

"Therefore also God highly exalted Him, and bestowed on Him the name which is above every name" (Phil. 2:9, NASB).

Because Christ humbled himself, God has highly exalted him, and his promise to us is that we are children of God, and "heirs also, heirs of God and fellow-heirs with Christ, if indeed we suffer with Him in order that we may be glorified with Him" (Rom. 8:17, NASB). God doesn't want to take away from me everything I've ever wanted. He wants to fulfill my innermost dreams.

Joanne Kanoff is a young wife and mother who became a believer in our fellowship. She says, "At first I cried at every service, until I finally realized I wasn't giving up anything worth having. Instead I found what I had really wanted all along!"

I've never met one who is a servant in the true sense who lacked a sense of fulfillment or wasn't getting his life together. This is a paradox the world cannot understand, but the point is that there are things in life you can't get by going after them. They come as a by-product of something else. Only the person who loves, and does not think of himself, actually finds himself. That is the great truth that we as a church have been called to demonstrate to the world.

The goal of the church is to present every person mature and complete in Christ—and the great characteristics of Christ are humility, obedience, and self-renunciation. In other words, Christian maturity ought to be marked by submission, and submission ought to be marked by joy.

By nature I am not submissive, and I am worse in the areas where I feel the least secure. As a young pastor I attended a seminar where the speaker said: "A common characteristic of evangelical pastors is their tendency to be defensive."

I spoke up, banging my fist on the table for emphasis, "We are not!" Everybody laughed at my "joke," but we all knew it held some truth.

Our first task as leaders is to encourage and build up our "younger" brothers and sisters in God's family.

My job is not to *make* anyone submit (although as an imperfect leader I sometimes try that with very unhappy results). In contrast, when I am able to regard someone else as more important than myself, I help that person sense his own worth as an individual. The person who knows he is accepted by God and others begins to desire to bend his will to God.

Christian growth takes place in the context of relationships, and the critical issue is always whether we're going to do things my way or your way. Anyone who seriously buckles down to learning to love by submitting is in for a few ego-shattering experiences. If you're tired of being a crabby, pessimistic, self-centered, lonely, and unhappy individual, try bending your will to others. Mutual servanthood has a way of polishing us until some of those good qualities God has given begin to shine through.

I have often said there ought to be a sign over every church door saying, "Danger, saints under construction." This isn't where the finished saints meet, but where they grow as they rub against each other.

Peter wrote, "You have become living building-stones for God's use in building his house" (1 Pet. 2:5, TLB). The house of God is not the building where you meet to worship; it is all of us, being built on the foundation of Jesus Christ, as a dwelling place for God himself.

A unique feature of this structure is its permanency. Everything else in creation—the stars, the moon, the sun, the planet earth, and all man's works—will end someday. The only thing that will still be around is the house God is building for himself by fitting our lives together in the church.

God's commitment to us is for all eternity; but when things get rough in our local group, our human tendency is to go look for another pile of living stones that might not require our ego to be chipped quite as much for us to fit in.

The problem is that without chipping, God can't shape us. Paul uses another illustration: "... we are to grow up in all aspects into Him, who is the head, even Christ, from whom the whole body, being fitted and held together by that which every joint supplies, according to the proper working of each individual part, causes the growth of the body for the building up of itself in love" (Eph. 4:15, 16, NASB).

We are growing and fitted and held together by something every joint supplies when it is working properly. A joint is where two or more bones come together so that they can work as one. It is in the joint that friction occurs. Joints are vital, but dangerous. When they don't work, we are stiff-legged, with unbending elbows or wrists.

What keeps the "joints" of our church body functioning without aches and pains is our willingness to submit to one another, and submission is seldom learned in short-term relationships. It is our lasting contact with others, who may be exasperating and demanding at times, that causes us to grow. God is the master builder who put us in exactly the spot he chose for us. We need the ones who rub against us, and they need us. To reject them may be to reject the very instrument God has chosen to develop us to full maturity in Christ Jesus.

My personal commitment to the local fellowship needs to be as long-lasting as I am able to make it. It is a recognition of my permanent relationship with God and others, and of my need for the discipline of the body system. I may be a near-perfect thumb or eye, but I'm not much good alone. Submission to the rest of the body is no threat to my individual freedom. I need to realize that I can't reach my full potential as a thumb or an eye unless I bend my will to the body I belong to.

I believe God has placed me as pastor/teacher in Salem, but I don't have an infallible view of what is to take place in the church, and therefore my gift needs to be augmented by the rest of the body. I sense more now than ever before that I need the discipline of working with others. I sometimes want to move too fast or try too much, and that is when God in his wisdom allows the executive committee or our elders to decide against my proposals. (As they did recently with a vote of thirteen to my one.)

It isn't easy, but I am learning the wisdom of listening to the rest of the staff, the elders, and the executive committee, because so often I sense God speaking to me through the body of the church.

The relationships of the staff and lay leaders become models for the rest of the fellowship. That is why the lists of qualifications for leaders do not mention skills or even spiritual gifts, but maturity in Christlike qualities. These are qualities everyone in the church should be maturing in, but since leaders are to be examples, growth should be evident in their lives.

On the five lists of qualifications for leaders in the New Testament are such personal qualities as: "above reproach, the husband of one wife, temperate, prudent, respectable, hospitable, able to teach, not addicted to wine or pugnacious [quarrelsome], but gentle, uncontentious, free from the love of money. He must be one who manages his own household well, keeping his children under control with all dignity (but if a man does not know how to manage his own household, how will he take care of the church of God?); and not a new convert, lest he become conceited and fall into the condemnation incurred by the devil. And he must have a good reputation with those outside the church, so that he may not fall into reproach and the snare of the devil" (1 Tim. 3:1-7, NASB).

With that kind of specifications, who in the world can be a leader? Remember, these are God's requirements in process, not in perfection. The most important thing is to see the process going on.

Leaders are imperfect people, and that should be evident to others as well as to ourselves. Knowing our limitations makes our need for each other more apparent. The growing pains in our staff relationships in Salem are so visible that people have remarked, "You're so different that we know you must have problems getting along . . . it's neat to see you love each other."

To see people who are different get along makes love believable. I've had someone tell me, "If you guys can work as a team, there's hope for the rest of us!"

The two most opposite people on our staff are still Ted and I, but there is evidence that we are being used to polish one another. Ted's desk is now often cleaner than mine, and I may be a little less harsh in demanding perfection of myself and others. When I lose my temper over a delayed report (as still happens on occasion), Ted is able to hear me out and say with unmistakable concern, "Don, you must really be hurting today. I'm sorry, I'll try to get that report in."

If Ted were to be defensive, trying to justify himself, I would very likely tense up more. Instead, his kind words take the edge off my frustration and I can see that my anger is harming us both.

Our staff meets each week to discuss the sermon thesis for the following Sunday. When it is my turn to preach, I count on Ted to drill me on the biblical soundness of my idea, since he has a better working knowledge of the Greek than I do. Sometimes the questions cut a little, but I know they will help me go into the pulpit, not just with a good idea, but with a sound one.

The sermon is the cutting edge of our ministry. Everything we hope to see happening in the church begins with what we believe God's Word has to say.

Even though we have hashed over the message in a staff meeting, we believe it is important to have feedback from the rest of the church. One way is through a Sermon Reflection class which meets during the Sunday school hour immediately following our first morning worship service. The members discuss what they received from the message, and the session is taped for careful review by the speaker.

There are always those who don't like what the pastor is saying, and often with good reason. Their ideas need to be expressed, and may be just the insight the pastor needs to make his point more clearly the next time.

After one of my messages a class member said, "That sermon made me furious!" From the comments of the class I could see that my presentation had not been clear enough. Over the years my sermons have become simpler and more direct. I am learning to share the truths I find in the Bible, starting from a point where it applies to my own life. I can say, "This is what I am learning from God's Word, and how I see it speaks to our lives."

In discipling others for leadership, it is hardest for me to learn when to push for results and when to let go. There is a fine balance between encouragement and pressure. One of the younger lay leaders in our fellowship is somewhat undisciplined. We had lunch together one day, and he apologized for something he had failed to get done on time. I sensed that he felt pressured and said, "I didn't invite you to lunch to get those things done. I wanted to have lunch with you because I enjoy our friendship."

He didn't look quite convinced, and I went on, "I know I've been urging you to get on with it, and I feel I may have pressured you into running from me. That is jeopardizing our friendship, and I apologize. Our relationship is more important than getting things done."

He smiled, relieved. "I have felt the pressure," he admitted. "And I've kind of avoided you. But I'm glad it's out in the open, and I want you to know that I sense strongly my responsibility for getting my task done."

As pastor/coach, it is my job to let a disciple know what is right in the Word of God and what is expected of him. When that is done, I am not to press, but let God the Holy Spirit do his work of prompting and enabling. My task from then on is to be encouraging and accepting. Slowly I am learning that I am not running the church. It is still God's work, and his church, and he is the builder and master coach.

Our executive committee must grapple with decisions about finance, buildings, and programs. I am convinced we would get hopelessly bogged down if we were not committed to one another and to Christ. The men come from a wide variety of backgrounds, economically, socially, and educationally. There is a wide age span, and some have been in the church more than twenty years, some for only two.

It is easy for me to feel defensive and pressured when some have a need to ask a lot of questions, but I am learning that I need to hear them, especially as the church is growing and requires expanded facilities, budgets, and programs.

Paul wrote, "And let the peace of Christ rule in your hearts, to which indeed you were called in one body; and be thankful" (Col. 3:15, NASB). Paul knew there are times when Christians disagree, and he chose a word for "rule" that also means "umpire." There will always be times when we pull in different directions. Can we submit our feelings of anger, defensiveness, or annoyance to Christ and let his peace be the umpire that settles the question? Then our differences will cease to be a threat, and instead provide the balance we need.

When a task force was assigned to draw up some guidelines for church policy, the members seemed poles apart. After two unfruitful meetings, we began the third session by reading from Jesus' prayer for his disciples.

"I do not ask in behalf of these alone, but for those also who believe in Me through their word; that they may be one, even as Thou, Father, art in Me, and I in Thee, that they also may be in Us" (John 17:20, 21, NASB).

The first basis of our unity in Christ is that we share a belief in the truth of his Word. We began our session by putting on the chalkboard things we believed together, by asking everyone to finish the sentence, "Jesus Christ is _____."

We went around the room, "Jesus Christ is truth . . . is totally

God and totally man . . . is the Lord of history . . . is the Lord of all . . . is my Savior . . . is the same yesterday, today, and forever."

Unmistakably the atmosphere lightened, and when we finished our list, someone began to sing a song of praise. As we all sang, we sensed the peace of Christ and the unity among us.

The business meeting that followed revealed that our differences were still there, but we were able to finish with total absence of antagonism, and with a testimony of our oneness in Christ. We had once been estranged; now we felt our closeness as brothers.

Our business meetings in the church usually begin with a time of sharing, centered around a passage of Scripture. The sharing helps us identify with one another, and is more meaningful when we are able to be honest about where we are in our process of being built together.

One executive committee meeting faced an agenda I had dreaded for some time. The chairman of the elders had just finished his first year on the committee, and was the first man to speak up:

"This has been the most difficult year of my life," he began. "I had never served on a board before, and the first three months my head was spinning. I didn't understand what you guys were talking about, and I felt angry and lost. I was almost going to quit. But I want you to know that God has pressed me to grow, and I have really learned some things."

The youngest member on the committee responded, "I started this year not very enthusiastic about my responsibilities, but I want you to know that you guys have really touched my life." He looked around the circle of faces, and the young man next to him punched his arm and said gruffly, "You dummy, you are going to make me cry, but I want to tell you it has meant a lot to me to watch you grow this year."

After an hour of sharing, praying, and thanking God for one another, our difficult business meeting took place in great harmony, although there was not agreement among us. Submitting to one another does not mean we will all agree, but the peace of Christ will rule our hearts.

119

At the close of a Sunday evening service, we sometimes observe the custom of "passing the peace." I turn to the men with me on the platform, shaking hands with each, saying: "Ted, may God's peace go with you this week." "Gene, may God's peace go with you this week." "Don, may God's peace go with you this week." Together we walk down the aisles, shaking hands with the first person in each pew, calling them by name, "May God's peace go with you this week." They turn to the person next to them with the same salutation, and as we move down the aisle, the peace of God is passed from one to the other through the entire fellowship. I can never get to the end of the aisle without crying. The peace of God brings an overwhelming sense of belonging to him and to one another.

As senior pastor coach, I am the principal mood-setter of our fellowship. If there is a wrong attitude among us, I need to first examine myself. We are to be a loving, caring, accepting family, marked by mutual submission. If the pastors don't love one another, or get along with the elders, our message of love from the pulpit will bear little fruit.

Christian leadership is being an example of growing in Christ-likeness. If I'm not maturing, no one will follow me into Christ-likeness. I may be an efficient organizer of a growing church, but if no one matures in his Christian life by following me, I'm not a Christian leader in the true sense of the word.

Some years ago I was rather exasperated with a young man in our church whom I will call Rick. I considered him bull-headed and inconsiderate, and he had hurt some people's feelings by rushing ahead with some things that should have been handled with patience. Most of all, I wanted to shake him and say, "Why don't you grow up!"

At that time I was studying Paul's letter to the Ephesians and preaching from the fourth chapter which says, "Be humble and gentle. Be patient with each other, making allowance for each other's faults, because of your love." Now that was something Rick really needed to learn, I thought. Perhaps, if I made an effort to be his friend, I could tell him.

It was in the fall of the year, and I needed firewood. Rick had mentioned he knew where to get some free wood, so rather than getting a cord of cut wood brought to the house for $20.00, I asked Rick, "How about taking me out to get some wood?"

"Sure." He looked eager. "I know a lady who has a cousin who owns some land, and I'll cut the wood and bring it to your house for you."

"I would enjoy going with you," I said. "I like being out in the woods this time of year."

Rick grinned. "Great, I don't go to work till noon, we can get out there and be back at your house in a couple of hours any day you want."

We agreed to go on Monday, on my day off, and Rick was at my house with his pickup truck before 7 A.M. On our way out of town I began to suspect that he had never been where we were going, and asked, "Did you call to say we were coming?"

My companion smiled confidently, "No, but it's OK. I have permission."

There was a gnawing unease in the back of my mind, but I said nothing as we swung off the road, down through an old orchard, to a heap of fallen oakwood bulldozed together. It was fine-looking wood, and in an hour the truck was loaded with half a cord. The exercise had done me good, and I breathed deeply in the air, fresh after the heavy rains.

We started up the grassy slope towards the pavement—and got stuck. Rick backed up and made another run—and we got stuck again. An hour later we were still backing up and trying.

My inward frustration was mounting—my anger too. Rick ought to have known better than to get off the road after the rain without four-wheel drive!

"Do you have towing insurance?"

He shook his head, and I was afraid I was going to lose my temper.

"I think we need to pray," I said with outward calm. "Then let's go over to that farmhouse and find someone to pull us out."

Rick glanced at me sideways as I bowed my head. "God, I don't understand what's going on, but I accept it as something from you."

The need to explode had left me, and at the farmhouse I introduced myself to the farmer's wife and told her we were cutting wood on so and so's property, and were stuck.

"That is not so and so's property." The lady wasn't smiling. "That's our property."

I didn't look at Rick and said, "Would you like to sell me half a cord of wood?"

She wasn't quite sure, but after some talking, I was allowed to pay $19.00 for the wood that hadn't really been for sale in the first place. It was almost twice the price per cord I would have paid to have it delivered.

Next we called a tow truck. When it arrived and I saw it was a small one, I asked the driver before he left the pavement if he thought he had adequate equipment to get us out.

"No problem." He looked almost a little hurt that I had raised the question. "If we need any help, I've got a two-way radio."

I watched him pull off the road, back into the orchard—and get stuck. After an hour of trying to get him out (the two-way radio wasn't working), we agreed it would be best to call a bigger tow truck to get us both out. It was almost noon, and Rick said, "I won't get to work on time anyway, so I'll go back to the farmhouse and make the call."

While he was gone, I was thinking, "God, I'm so upset. What in the world are you trying to do?" To my fuming head came the quiet thought, "Perhaps God is trying to teach you something."

I was almost calm when Rick came back with the news that the second tow truck was out on call and couldn't get there for another hour.

With amazing restraint I said, "You've got to get to work, and I've got a lot to do today, and this is frustrating to both of us. So I think we need to ask God to give us the right answer about it."

We prayed and sat there talking, when Rick said, "You know Pastor, this is really a significant day for me."

"How's that?" I looked at my young friend and his eyes were lit up.

"I've always wondered how you would react under pressure."

"I've come close to blowing it," I admitted, and Rick nodded. "Me, too, but it's really neat to see you in a tough spot like this."

I was thanking God for keeping my lid on when the second tow truck arrived. It was big—but it got stuck. Now there were three trucks in line on the slick slope. The big truck had a wench, and by fastening the cable around a fruit tree, we were able to move a few yards at a time. One tree looked rotten, and I said, "Are you sure it will hold?" "Sure," said the driver, and a few seconds later the old tree went *kerplunk*.

It took us an hour to make the 200 yards to the pavement. Rick and I had started up the slope five hours earlier.

At the garage I was charged only $50.00 for the two trucks, since I *had* pointed out to the driver that his equipment might not be adequate. The total cost for my "free wood" was $69.00, which I was able to pay without a sense of great loss. The day had turned out to be a meaningful experience.

On the way to my house, Rick said, "You know, today has been a real happening. I've learned something."

"So have I," I said. "It wasn't an easy thing, but I'm glad we went through it together."

The final scene of that day's comedy of errors came when I was told that someone had broken into the church that morning and stolen some office supplies. The sexton didn't hide his smile when he said, "I understand that while the church was broken into, you were out stealing wood!"

Being an example is an awesome thing. God in his sovereignty has chosen to place this kind of responsibility on human beings, not because we are perfect, but because we are people in the process of becoming more Christlike.

The very fact that we aren't perfect makes the process more evident. My own failures make me aware of my inadequacy and dependence on Christ. I could easily have lost my temper with Rick that memorable day, and I think it was evident to him that his pastor was not a patient man but that God gave him patience.

The greatest need in the church is for mutual servanthood, but it begins with the elders. We don't teach submission by demanding that others yield to us, but by submitting to them. If our attitude of servanthood is genuine, others will sense more of their own worth, and will be given the desire to follow in submission.

All along, Jesus was trying to communicate to his disciples that the way to find life is to give it up, the way to use authority is to submit, and the key to being a leader is to master servanthood.

"They will know you are my disciples because you love one another," Jesus said. Mature Christian love is expressed in mutual servanthood. A church where this is in process will be an accepting and loving fellowship where we find ourselves by giving ourselves.

11
I Hear You Say
You Love Me

Loving someone can be hard work sometimes, and some aspects of it are more difficult than others. It is like taking care of the yard, which is my job at home. I like mowing better than picking weeds. Mowing takes about thirty minutes of steady, hard work, but even if it makes me perspire, I know that when it is done, I'm through for a week. Weeding, on the other hand, goes on and on, and you never quite get done.

God has already established our pattern for loving one another. He demonstrated it when he chose to accept us and love us, although we can do nothing to deserve it. He is committed to loving us, and our failures can't stop him. He forgives and goes on loving, no matter what.

It is wonderful to be in a fellowship where we are learning to love one another like that. Learning to accept difficult people and allow them the freedom to be different—encouraging and forgiving them when they step on our toes—isn't easy, but it is still the easiest part, the mowing of the yard. I'd rather do it than picking weeds.

Loving gets more difficult when it requires us to face up to the reality of right and wrong. That is the kind of love parents must show when Johnny insists on playing in the middle of a busy street. They don't stop loving him because he plays there, but their love requires them to say, "Johnny, this is not where you play, or you're going to be hit by a car. So we are going to spank you to save you from something far worse."

God has shown us that quality of love from the very beginning, through his prophets and later, his Son. He says: "Look, I love you, and nothing can change my works of love, but my standards are righteousness and justice, and unless you meet them, there will be some hard consequences." That is reality.

One of the men in our fellowship says, "You can't put all the emphasis on acceptance and friendship. At some point you have to say, 'This is the line, beyond which is trouble.' "

To know that there is absolute truth, and to align our lives with that truth, gives the Christian a sense of security and of freedom as well. Engineers are careful to align their construction of airplanes with the absolute laws of aerodynamics. Absolute truth does not limit our freedom; it shows us how to be free within the scope of reality.

"If you abide in My word, then you are truly disciples of Mine; and you shall know the truth, and the truth shall make you free," said Jesus (John 8:31, 32). He also said, "I am the truth."

Helping each other face up to reality is a difficult, but a loving thing to do.

If I speak the truth because it makes me feel a little holier than the person I am speaking to, I am not qualified to utter the words that are burning my tongue. In fact, a burning tongue is often a sign that my attitude is less than loving. I need to ask myself if I am speaking the truth to build up my brother, or my own ego. If there is a trace of condemnation or judgment in my attitude, I will be tearing him down instead.

A friend of mine once spoke to a sister in the church about her tendency to gossip. At the end of their conversation, my friend asked: "What did you hear me say just now?" The sister answered, "I heard you say you love me!"

If we say, "Brother, I need to tell you this in love . . ." but our unspoken attitude communicates that we see him as a failure, our words of truth will do more harm than good. (Unless our brother is more mature than we are, and able to absorb the sting of our words.)

It is a weakness of mine to be impatient with other people's

126

weaknesses. My first impulse to speak is often tainted by mixed motives. In order to check myself, I sometimes first express my frustration on paper, and then, with my motives somewhat purer, I am able to speak in a more helpful way.

At one point I was quite upset with a leader in the church because his committee was behind schedule. I had sense enough to know that I was unable to speak the truth in an encouraging way. Instead, I wrote the man a note I did not intend to mail. At the top of the page I put: "This is what I *feel*." Then I wrote:

"Dear brother: I have mixed feelings of hurt and frustration. You and I used to be close. I feel you are not interested in matters that are your primary responsibility in the church. Am I seeing it wrong? Are you responding out of hurt and frustration over my impatience?"

Putting that note aside, I could write an encouragement card saying, "Brother, I really miss you . . . Love, Don."

The next day I avoided direct confrontation with him, and the following day we were together in a committee meeting. He contributed a real insight to our discussion, and I expressed appreciation for that. The next day I wrote another encouragement card, thanking him again for what he had said. By then my feelings of frustration were diminished, and so was my need to tell him where he was wrong.

To speak the truth in love is my responsibility as a Christian, but in my humanness, the urge to speak is not always prompted by a spirit of love. Being slow to speak is a good way to filter our words, while praying much for God to purify our motives.

It is the Holy Spirit in us that confronts the world with the truth about Jesus Christ. My part is to come in humility to my brother. The Holy Spirit will make him see his wrong without me having to spell it out for him (John 16:8). Often a question will prompt our brother to think through his situation for himself.

A young man had been elected to an office in the fellowship, but when summer came and school let out, he and his family seldom came to church on Sunday. I saw him one day, and said: "We miss seeing you on a regular basis on Sundays."

His smile was a little hesitant. "I feel my first responsibility is to my family, and the kids need the experience of camping out during the summer."

"I agree that your first responsibility is to your family," I said. "But I just want to ask you this: are you entirely satisfied with your choice of handling that responsibility for the summer?"

He looked at me, then said a little curtly, "I'm satisfied."

"That's all I want to know." We chatted briefly, and parted with a warm handshake.

Before long the family were in church regularly on Sunday again, and the young man told me, "The last time we talked, you didn't pressure me to come to church, but I couldn't get away from your question. You see, I wasn't *really* satisfied with camping every weekend, and you sort of confronted me with it, while giving me the freedom to make my own decision."

I am not always so tactful. One Sunday morning I saw Brad Coleman and a friend leave the church building during the Sunday school hour, heading for the coffee shop. Brad was Assistant Sunday School Superintendent at the time, and there was always the possibility he would be needed during the class session. Just as I was getting ready to go into the second worship service, I ran into Brad and his friend coming back from their little expedition.

Fighting to control myself, I said, "I hope you weren't going where I thought you were going when I saw you leave!"

They looked like schoolboys caught skipping a class, and I lost my control, fairly yelling down the hall. My outburst caught them by surprise. Brad, who caught the brunt of my displeasure, looked hurt and embarrassed. By now I was angry with both of us, and hurried into the service with an urgent, "Help! I failed again!" directed heavenward.

Later I was able to say to Brad, "Will you accept my apology for speaking the way I did?"

He grinned and took my outstretched hand. "I guess we both blew it," he said. "It was a dumb thing to do."

Years later Brad told me that my apology had made a greater impression than my anger. "You thought enough of me to say you were sorry—even if I had been wrong. It made me feel better about making a mistake. I learned that pastors make them too, and have to apologize like the rest of us."

Our truth-speaking is less likely to be misunderstood when we have first established a relationship of love. This kind of open, accepting relationship allows us to remove our pretenses and see each other as less than perfect. Then we can say to one another, "How do you see me? Do I talk too much, or too harshly? Do I come across as critical or self-centered?" To answer less than honestly is to be less than loving. Truth, spoken in love, helps us see ourselves more clearly, and helps us grow.

Sometimes a painful truth is the most loving thing we can say to someone. I know, because I have had them said to me. One of the men on the executive committee called one day and invited me for lunch. Before we went out to eat, he said, "I need to talk to you."

"Go ahead."

He cleared his throat. "I need to be honest with you, Don. I see you pressing so-and-so too hard. You are just frustrating him. I know you don't mean to, but you do."

I felt uncomfortable, but it was clear that my friend felt even worse. Thanking him, I said, "I know this was a tough thing to do, but it tells me that you love me, or you wouldn't have taken the risk of confronting me."

My friend helped me see how others saw me. That can be both an encouraging and difficult thing to face. I have learned to ask frequently in conversations, "What do you hear me say?" And I often summarize what others say to me: "This is what I understand you are saying . . ."

Most of us have the habit of speaking before we've thought something through. Hearing our own words echoed back to us can be helpful and sometimes surprising.

At a board meeting, one of the men expressed vaguely negative feelings about an upcoming project he was assigned to lead. I felt he needed to get his feelings out into the open, so that he could honestly say no to a task he did not want to do.

I said, "Brother, I heard you, and it helps me to see that you don't really want to do this thing."

He looked surprised. "Is that what you heard me say?"

He looked thoughtful, and later told me, "I've come to realize that I really *do* want that challenge. Thanks for helping me see my indecisiveness." He headed up the project with zest and with excellent results.

To become a whole person, as God plans for us, we need the relationship with those who love us enough to help us face ourselves as we are.

A middle-aged housewife had been on the verge of a nervous breakdown when she first came to our church. She faced problems at home in her relationships with her husband and children, but her biggest problem was herself. She began to attend a Wednesday night study and sharing group, where she found freedom to talk about how she really felt about things.

"I was sometimes angry, upset, or negative," she said. "But they weren't threatened. They listened to me, prayed for me, and pointed out my blind spots; but it was such a gentle form of reproof. Never in my life had I been reproved any way but harshly. I brought my whole muddled up mess of a life in there and they cared enough not to talk about it outside the group. They really loved me."

Because she felt the overwhelming sense of her friends' love, she was able to take their gentle reproof without feeling threatened.

When we are angry or hurt, we need someone who can quietly listen while we vent our negative feelings. I am learning that in God's sovereign will, he has put us together, the one who needs to speak and the one who needs to listen.

After a Sunday evening service, I invited a new couple to go with us to the Friendship Hour. The man said, "Yes, we'd like to, but I need to talk to you first." There was urgency in his voice. I sat down next to him in the pew. He tried to speak several times, but was overcome with emotion.

I said, "Just wait, and let this pass."

His wife took their two young children and went to the nursery to fetch their youngest one, and the man said, "I'm so upset about this film tonight!"

We had shown a film about the danger of violence on television, and the film had contained some scenes of violence that were examples of this.

"There was no nursery for our three- and four-year-olds, and they saw things in church tonight that we would never let them watch at home."

His anger and frustration spilled over in tears as he said, "The church ought to have provided something for the little ones to do."

His words hit me. My children were old enough to handle the film, but to expose the little ones . . . it was an oversight I needed to be told about.

"Thanks for making me aware of the situation," I said. "I am really very sorry we hadn't thought about it."

He smiled suddenly. "Man, I feel so good having expressed this; I just feel free!"

The Bible says, "Where the Spirit of the Lord is, there is freedom." It is an essential ingredient in a loving fellowship. It needs to be encouraged, even to some degree in our services, our classes, and groups—not to the exclusion of careful planning, but so that we are open and sensitive to what God wants to do. That can be risky, because it means that sometimes someone will say something that is irrelevant or should have been left unsaid.

On Sunday evenings when our church family meets for sharing and prayer, some of us get a little nervous at times. It is obvious that none of us has a tight control of the situation. This is as it should be, because it serves as a reminder that it isn't the senior pastor, but Jesus Christ, who is the Head of the church. Only when the Holy Spirit is in control can we have the kind of freedom that involves risk . . . and trust that the real Boss will work through us to handle any situation that appears difficult.

I was concerned when old Tom, in his eighties, stood up several Sunday evenings in a row to share at length his memories from childhood. I finally cut him off as gently as I could, and said to the congregation, "Family, it is important for us to have this kind of open sharing, and it requires a lot of love to absorb someone like Tom who is not always relevant." Tom's beaming face told me that he was not offended by my words, but rather enjoyed our concern.

Later we talked it over in staff, and Gene French, our associate pastor, said, "I sense that Tom is getting up to talk because he is a lonely old man who needs attention."

I mentioned what Gene had said to Marvin Woods, the chairman of our elders. Marvin was to open the next Sunday night service with prayer, and I suggested, "Perhaps it would be good if you could sit by Tom and help him."

Marv said, "I'm not so sure I can handle that, but I'll try."

Tom was sitting at the end of a pew, and I saw Marv get a folding chair and sit next to him in the aisle. When the sharing began, another dear brother, who sometimes says things that aren't too relevant, got up to ask prayer for an aunt.

"Who wants to stand and respond?" I invited, and nobody did right away. Then Marv stood and prayed, and said, "Before I return the microphone, I'd just like to share with the family a word from my brother Tom and me. We've talked it over, and decided that neither of us is going to share tonight. We will give our time so that other people can have an opportunity to share."

Tom nodded his smiling approval.

It had been a gentle form of discipline, insuring both Tom's freedom to speak, and the orderliness of the service.

The story has an interesting sequel. The fellowship has by now accepted Tom as someone who is quite senile at times, but who has a very firm faith and deep commitment to Jesus Christ. Our elders arrange for people to lead the invocation Sunday night, and recently Roger Fisher told me, "I've asked Tom to do the opening prayer tonight."

When I told Gene French who was leading that part of the service, he said, "Are you serious?" I assured him I was, but while the congregation was singing, I could see that Gene was struggling, and so was I. Neither one of us knew what Tom would do.

When the singing was over, Gene asked him to come forward, and some of the people looked surprised. Tom stood before the microphone, and prayed a very short, beautiful prayer. He did it very gently, and pointedly, and it was a moving thing for us all.

Later a teen-ager said to me, "The kids thought it was really neat when Tom prayed."

As a church, our goal is to present each of us mature and whole in Christ. That means we aren't there yet, and in our humanness we sometimes need to be disciplined.

The words *disciple* (learner) and *discipline* come from the same root. The learning process requires discipline, and the church that makes disciples must be a disciplining church:

"Let God train you, for he is doing what any loving father does for his children. Whoever heard of a son who was never corrected? For when he punishes you, it proves that he loves you" (Heb. 12:7, 6, TLB).

A church that is learning to discipline in love will be a strong church. Bernie Chipman, a young housewife in our fellowship, says, "I think that's why I feel so secure in this church. Like in a family. The love includes authority, direction, and discipline. We know what God is saying, and what he expects of us. We're not just doing our own thing."

Without discipline, our love is not complete. And without love, discipline destroys instead of building up. Our fellowship is a call to mutual love and submission, and there is no greater challenge to that call than when a member of the body strays from God's truth.

Historically, the church has a poor record of loving discipline (probably due in part to the most glaring mistakes getting the most publicity). We must acknowledge shameful things like the Inquisition, burnings at the stake, and persecutions. All were performed by those who claimed to be guardians of the truth. In contrast, some modern churches have leaned over backward in permissiveness, to the point of failing to affirm the absolute nature of God's truth.

In evangelical churches, where we hold the Bible as our authority, we sometimes try to avoid the issue by looking the other way when we first become aware of someone wandering from the truth. If the wrong reaches scandalous proportions we are forced to excommunicate the culprit to save the reputation of our fellowship.

Our reluctance to administer discipline is understandable. Many evangelical groups have gained a reputation as "narrow-

133

minded legalists," who are fond of rules and regulations. Our critics frequently quote Jesus' words, "Judge not, or you will be judged," and we don't want to be guilty of that!

I think our problem stems from our tendency to confuse the sinner with his sins, or the doer with the deed. God *loves* the sinner while condemning his sin, but we constantly make the mistake of condemning the person along with his wrong deeds. It is equally a mistake to think that we must love the sins along with the sinner. The most loving thing Jesus did was to separate us from our sins. He took our sins upon himself on the cross so that we could be free from the penalty of being eternally bound to them.

It is true that we are never to judge one another's worth, but the Bible tells us to correct one another when we wander from God's truth. Paul wrote: "If a man should be detected in some sin, my brothers, the spiritual ones among you should quietly set him back on the right path, not with any feeling of superiority, but being yourselves on guard against temptation. Help one another to carry these heavy loads, and so live out the law of Christ" (Gal. 6:1, paraphrased).

In the Greek text, the word for "setting him back on the right path," is "equip." Discipline is part of the equipping we all need at times, and its purpose is to strengthen and restore, not condemn or destroy.

The responsibility for setting a wanderer back on the right path is given to "the spiritual ones" among us. I understand that to refer to the elders in the fellowship, not individually, but collectively. Here is one case in which there is safety in numbers. In our humanness, no one of us alone is capable of judging whether someone else is straying from the truth. If we sense that a brother or sister is on the wrong track, we are to take it to an elder, and the elders together are to submit the matter in prayer to the Head of the church, Jesus Christ, asking for wisdom.

Jesus, who knew the church would be made up of imperfect people, advised his disciples: "If a brother sins against you, go to him privately and confront him with his fault. If he listens and confesses it, you have won back a brother. But if not, then take one or two others with you, and go back to him again, proving everything you say by these witnesses. If he still refuses to listen, then take your case to the church, and if the church's verdict favors you, but he won't accept it, then the church should excommunicate him" (Matt. 18:15-17, TLB).

In our Salem fellowship the elders deal with the matters of discipline. I am only involved as their coach and fellow elder. No other aspect of leadership requires as much awareness of our humanness and God's grace. I love the 89th Psalm which says: "If my children forsake my laws and don't obey them, I will punish them, but I will never completely take away my lovingkindness from them, nor let my promise fail" (vv. 30-33, TLB).

Before we can go in love to someone who is doing wrong, we must sense that no matter what they have done, or how we may feel about it, God has not removed his lovingkindness from them, and neither must we. God's purpose for discipline is always restoration, and we can never forget that.

Often an elder must wrestle with his own critical feelings, and find forgiveness for them, before he is ready to speak to a wandering brother or sister in a spirit of gentleness that says, "I see you are hurting, let me help you face up to this thing in your life."

The wanderer may be defensive and critical of our judgment. Our task is not to tell him what he already knows in his heart, but to give him the encouragement and support he needs to confess his wrong and turn from it.

When a wanderer is brought into fellowship, the restoration should be complete. President Lincoln was asked how he intended to treat the rebellious Southerners once they were defeated and returned to the union of the United States. Lincoln said, "I shall treat them as if they had never been away."

In the parable of the prodigal son, Jesus shows us the picture of God as the loving Father who waits with open arms for the errant child to return home. He speaks no word of rebuke, or "I told you so." His is a love that forgives and never mentions the wrong again. That is our pattern.

When our elders have to confront people in love, the situation most often remains a very private one between one or two elders and the person who needed help.

135

Over the years we've had our share of teen-age marriages at Salem. Some young couples who have been very sincere in their commitment to one another nevertheless have found themselves facing a premarital pregnancy. We don't consider pregnancy sufficient grounds for marriage, and a counseling pastor will attempt to make certain that the couple share a deep commitment to each other and to Christ before we will agree to marry them.

The case will be discussed by our elders, and one or two men will meet with the couple to help them face up to their situation in light of God's Word. Usually the young people are greatly relieved to deal with their guilt before God in the presence of the elders who accept and forgive them.

When other young people in the church are aware of the situation, there is often unspoken embarrassment and a strain on the relationships. In such a case, the elders will suggest that the matter be dealt with openly before those who are directly concerned. It is difficult, but sometimes necessary to say to those we have hurt: "We have violated God's law and yours. We have confessed our sin to him, and we need to confess it to you. We have asked God's forgiveness, and now we ask yours."

Such a confession is painful, but always brings a release and restoration of the relationship between the young couple and their friends. Once their sin has been confessed and forgiven, they are free to be open and honest with each other. The invisible wall of suspicion, embarrassment, and pretending is removed.

Only once have we found it necessary to excommunicate a brother from the fellowship. It was a case of adultery in which the husband moved out to live with another woman. When confronted by first his elder, then a pastor, he did not want to speak to them. He no longer attended the church, and he made it clear that he would continue in his new life-style.

Without mentioning the man's name, the elder reported the case to the board, and after prayer it was agreed to send the man a letter, which in essence said:

> *Dear brother:*
>
> *As we understand the Word of God, you are violating the biblical principles concerning marriage . . .*

We sense an unwillingness on your part to speak to us about it, and as we understand the Word of God, we are required to deal with it. At our next elders meeting, the coming Tuesday, we will recommend that you be dismissed from membership. You are welcome to the meeting to discuss it with us then.

We want you to know that we believe the loving thing for us to do is to confront you with what we see to be the violation of God's truth. We do it in the hope that you will turn in repentance and faith to God who forgives and redeems us.

This is not done with a view to permanent dismissal, but with a hope of your restoration to our fellowship.

We are looking forward to the time when you will come to talk to us about these things.   *Your brothers.*

Paul found it necessary to instruct the church in Corinth to excommunicate a brother who persisted in violating God's truth (1 Cor. 5). Some time later, Paul wrote, "He has been punished enough by your united disapproval. Now it is time to forgive him and comfort him" (2 Cor. 2:6, 7, TLB).

The purpose of discipline is always redemption. A loving fellowship is accepting, encouraging, and caring. It loves by facing up to reality and it disciplines, and it forgives and restores the returning wanderer. To present every one mature in Christ requires a love that is willing to pick the weeds and prune the bushes as well as mow the lawn.

Jesus said: "I am the true Vine, and my Father is the Gardener. He lops off every branch that doesn't produce. And he prunes those that bear fruit for even larger crops. He has already tended you by ... means of the commands I gave you. Take care to live in me, and let me live in you. For a branch can't produce fruit when severed from the vine. Nor can you be fruitful apart from me" (John 15:1-4, TLB).

Our relationship with God in Christ is described in many ways in the Bible. Christ is the head—we his body. He is the cornerstone—we the building. He is the vine—we the branches. God is the loving Father—we his children. Always the picture illustrates our dependency on him and our need to yield ourselves to the Father's hand.

God is the Gardener, the Builder, the Father, the Disciplinarian. It is neither our authority nor our truth that can bring anyone to turn from rebellion to faith. We are to yield ourselves in mutual submission to God and each other. Then the loving, maturing church can also be a disciplining church, used of God as an instrument of grace and reconciliation in a rebellious and troubled world.

12
The Witnessing Church

Some years ago I heard Dr. Richard Halverson say that "when people are in the right relationship with God and with one another, evangelism happens spontaneously, consistently, and almost effortlessly."

Getting things organized and functioning smoothly are the housekeeping chores that must be attended to so that love can happen in the church. The goal of Christian service isn't hard work, but God has wisely arranged it so that work is necessary.

Our love relationship with God and one another develops as we work together, and as new believers are drawn to our fellowship we are challenged to work and grow together more.

With nearly fifteen hundred people under pastoral care, we recently voted to establish twenty-one neighborhood sub-parishes throughout the city of Salem. Each sub-parish is headed by an elder, a deacon, and a deaconess. They are to lead by example, and by training the others to minister to one another. Each sub-parish will choose a form of monthly get-together: a backyard picnic, a Bible study, or some other event. The purpose of the division is to forge this mini-church into a caring group that can minister more effectively to its members whether the need is a flat tire, sickness, or other problem.

The goal of the church is to produce mature, Christlike people, and this spiritual growth process is greatly facilitated by our learning to minister together and to one another.

Since early childhood most of us have heard the words of Jesus: "But you shall receive power when the Holy Spirit has come upon you, and you shall be My witnesses both in Jerusalem and in all Judea and Samaria, and even to the remotest part of the earth" (Acts 1:8, NASB). I always thought that meant we were to go out and tell everybody about Jesus, but there came a day when I discovered that Jesus wasn't giving a command; he was stating a fact. Witnessing is not what we *do*, it is what we *are*, spilling over into what we do and say. Jesus was saying that when he lives in us through the power of the Holy Spirit, then our entire life-style will tell of him, wherever Christians scatter throughout the whole world. Christ in us, the hope of glory, shining through so that the world can see who he is and what he can do: that is what we are supposed to be witnesses of.

The goal of the church is to know Christ better, and so grow in his likeness—that through our lives we will make him known. That was how the early church spread the gospel. They didn't organize mass campaigns, set quotas and goals, and develop methods for soul-winning. But the gospel spread wherever Christians went, because the church—their special relationship to God and each other—was so healthy that the world could see the life of Christ in them.

Evangelism has always been an urgent concern of mine, because I understand the Word of God to say that he wants the whole world to know him, and he wants to use us to do it. My first sermon in Salem was on practicing hospitality to nonbelievers in order to win their friendship and introduce them to Christ. That's when I discovered that we can't be hospitable to strangers until we learn to be hospitable to each other. We work on both, but I have learned that any strategy for evangelism or witnessing must focus on nurturing the relationships or the *koinonia* in the church.

Of all the so-called methods of reaching people for Christ, none are as effective as his own. He simply loved people and accepted them. He was their Friend. In friendship evangelism, you make friends with people and so introduce them to Jesus, their Friend, who lives in you.

From the start in Salem, we provided some special opportunities to invite a friend to a social function. Most people who are strangers to the church are a little hesitant to come to the church building at first. They feel more at ease when they are brought to a ladies' friendship luncheon or men's fellowship breakfast at a restaurant in town. Small groups meeting in homes also make it easier to include those who aren't familiar with the church.

Even with structured friendship happenings, we found that most people are fearful of taking the risk of inviting someone they don't know very well. John and Carole Meyers said: "It took us four years to get up the nerve to invite someone. We were afraid they'd turn us down. Now we are getting brave enough to invite a couple of people every chance we get."

An open survey in the church revealed that most of us felt the same way. The survey was designed to establish what people believed about evangelism and what they were doing about it.

People were asked to indicate how frequently they made social contacts with non-Christians and give true/false statements to such questions as:

"Evangelism should primarily take place in a church service."

"Christians should not be friends with non-Christians."

"When non-Christians do not maintain your moral standards, it is important that they be corrected immediately."

"Telling people the gospel is more important than loving them."

The majority of the people had a good understanding of the nature of evangelism. Several said things like: "Evangelism is loving people for Christ." "It is communicating the gospel by how we live and what we say." "It is being a friend."

In contrast, the score on making contacts with non-Christians was miserably low, just as it had been in our surveys on hospitality and greeting strangers.

Openly admitting our fearfulness makes it easier to deal with. We can begin to encourage one another, remembering that Christ in us is always able to love others. Launching out in faith, we find our timidity lessened.

We remind ourselves that the world outside is a lonely place where people hunger for the genuine relationships we are finding in God's family. Turn on any radio station, and what you hear may be hard rock or Cole Porter, but the message is the same. It talks of loneliness and a need for love. If we can penetrate people's disguises, we find a deep hunger for relationships —to be accepted and loved by someone.

Paul wrote on this subject: "Conduct yourselves with wisdom toward outsiders, making the most of the opportunity. Let your speech always be with grace, seasoned, as it were, with salt, so that you may know how you should respond to each person" (Col. 4:5, 6, NASB).

"Outsiders" are those who have not believed in Jesus Christ, and because they have not believed, the Word of God says they are already condemned. This places a tremendous responsibility on those of us who do believe.

The Christians in Colossae to whom Paul wrote were a distinct minority in a city of commerce and intellectual awareness. Their lives would be watched by the "outsiders," and Paul told them first of all to be wise in their conduct. James described the wisdom that comes from God: [It] is first of all pure and full of quiet gentleness. Then it is peace-loving and courteous. It allows discussion and is willing to yield to others; it is full of mercy and good deeds. It is wholehearted and straightforward and sincere" (Jas. 3:17, TLB).

Few can be that kind of witness in perfection, but remember that Christian maturing is a process, and these qualities ought to be noticeably developing in us.

Some Christians are neither wise nor courteous as they shout or wave their placards: "I'm a fool for Christ, who are you a fool for?" They are anxious to promote their own ideas, and have neither concern or thought for the opinions of others.

While speaking at a seminar on friendship evangelism in another city, I was invited to the home of a Christian woman. I had been told by one of the other guests that this woman's husband was not a believer, and that she hoped our visit would influence him.

As we stepped inside the door of the home, there stood a large, two-foot-by-three-foot rack holding tracts on salvation. Above it was a sign in bold letters, "Repent or Perish!"

142

I suddenly felt great sympathy for the man who had to see that every time he opened the door to his own house. His wife was probably sincere enough in her desire to communicate the love of Christ to him, but she was going about it in a very unwise way. Peter had this word of advice to wives of unbelievers: " . . . be submissive to your own husbands, so that even if any of them are disobedient to the Word, they may be won without a word by the behavior of their wives" (1 Pet. 3:1, NASB).

The wise conduct that is a witness for Christ is straightforward and sincere; it is honest and above reproach. A lot of folks who know we are Christians watch our ethics very carefully. Do we cheat just a little? Stretch the speed limit? Call in sick when it is convenient? I know that God looks at what is in our hearts, but those who are outside can only judge by appearances.

A few years ago, a new family moved next door to Gene and Betty French. Ned Kanoff drove a beer truck, and he and his wife Joanne weren't too happy to discover that their neighbors were a pastor's family.

"I thought they'd be watching us," Joanne said later. "I didn't know much about Christians, and I thought Betty would disapprove if I drank coffee or cokes."

One day Gene was mowing his half of the grass between the two driveways. He thought he would be neighborly and mow the other half as well, so he took the hose Ned had left on the grass and threw it over on the walk. The end of the hose hit a tiny rhododendron, knocking off its only bud and two of its three leaves. Gene thought, "Oh, no! I'll have to tell Ned what I've done to his plant." Then he reasoned, "It's such an insignificant plant, I'll just keep quiet."

Two days later Ned was mowing his lawn, and Betty and Gene were outside. Gene was washing the car and Betty was working in the flower bed. She asked Ned what happened to his little rhododendron, and he replied, "Oh, one of the girls must have damaged it while they were playing."

Gene's ears were burning as he thought to himself, "If you want to be a witness to this neighbor, you should admit your fault." Then he checked himself, "What would Ned think of me if he knew I was responsible and didn't tell him earlier?"

A week or so later, Betty and Gene were visiting Ted and Edna Zabel, when Ted told of an incident that happened ten years earlier, involving a rosebush and negligence on his part. It had been a struggle to finally admit his fault to the owner. While Ted was talking, Gene was becoming convinced that this was God's way of reminding him that he ought to confess his own wrong to his neighbor. He shared the entire story with Ted and Edna, and the following Saturday he found an opportunity to tell Ned and ask his forgiveness. He also offered to replace the rhododendron.

On Sunday morning Ned decided to visit our church, along with Joanne and their two little daughters. In the Welcome Class I asked the question: "What is one thing you have learned this week?" and Ned quickly replied, "I learned that preachers are human like the rest of us."

Gene's honesty about his humanness helped Ned recognize the life of Christ in his neighbor. When he changed jobs and quit working on Sundays, the entire Kanoff family began coming to church on a regular basis, and today they are enthusiastic members of our growing family.

Not only our conduct, but our speech is to be gracious, kind, and courteous, communicating to others the grace of God. Paul said our speech was to be "seasoned, as it were, with salt, so that you may know how you should respond to each person." Salt implies flavor; it isn't flat and insipid. Another obvious thing about salt is that it creates a thirst.

Some of us try to give people a three-hour indoctrination course to Christianity the first time we meet them. If they hear us out, they'll be so saturated they will never want to hear more. If we give them only a few tasty morsels, we'll just whet their appetite.

When I give a sermon or a talk, I'd rather have people tell me, "You should have kept talking..." than to have them imply, "You should have stopped twenty minutes ago!" That's when I know I didn't make them thirsty... I drowned them.

Several years ago I climbed on a plane for Chicago and found my assigned window seat. A gray-haired, well dressed gentleman was seated on the aisle seat. I asked if the window seat was taken, and he replied a little gruffly, "Obviously not."

I carried my attaché case in one hand and an overnight bag in the other, and as I tried to get to my seat, I stepped on his foot. When I was seated, he deliberately dusted off his shoe, and I apologized profusely, but it didn't seem to make him any happier.

Several times during the flight I tried to start a conversation, but he didn't respond. Finally we were nearing Chicago, and I asked him where he was going.

"To Europe."

"Is it your first trip?"

"No, it's my seventh."

I said, "I don't know what you do, but whatever it is, you must be doing it well, to go to Europe for the seventh time. What *do* you do?"

"I don't do anything."

"You must do it very well." I tried smiling, and he didn't smile back, so I continued talking. "A person like you must be quite successful in life. I'd like to ask you a question."

"Yes?"

"What do you think the purpose of life is?"

He looked hard at me and said, "I really don't know for sure what life is all about, but if you are one of those people who is trying to witness to me by citing the 'four spiritual laws,' I have a nephew like that, and I don't want to hear it."

While I pondered that one, he said, "What do *you* do?"

I cleared my throat. "Well, I'm one of those preachers that goes around stepping on people's toes."

He laughed, and I noticed the tag on his attaché case; it was a well-known name in Oregon. I said, "Isn't it your family that has given the stadium to the university?"

He said, "Yes," and proceeded to tell me what was wrong with the church. "A bunch of lifeless hypocrites who have religion without meaning."

When I said, "I agree with that," he looked a little surprised, and I went on to say that I had committed my life to the church, because when it really *is* the church, it is the most exciting thing in the world. I told him briefly some of the things we were discovering together in Salem about our relationship with God and each other. By that time we landed in Chicago, and I gave him my card.

"If you're ever in Salem and need a free lunch, call me. I'd love to see you again."

He thanked me and said he'd like that. When I got home I wrote him a note, and he responded with a warm, handwritten letter thanking me for my friendship.

I thanked the Father for letting me be a friend to that man, and a witness for Jesus Christ, that day.

It is a fact of life that the unevangelized of the world are not especially interested in hearing our message, but they can't help being curious when they sense Jesus himself living in the messenger.

To act wisely is to develop friendships with nonbelievers. That is how most of the newcomers are added to our fellowship. Most of us who are believers today can look back on the time when we first felt a drawing toward Jesus Christ. There was someone in our life who was a believer, and who took an interest in us.

The person who tries to win the whole world misses everybody. It is best to concentrate our efforts on building friendships with specific people.

Ask God to point out those special people to you. They may be very natural contacts; relatives, your neighbors, someone at work, at school, or maybe the clerk where you do your shopping. Write down their names and pray daily for them. Don't pray simply that God will save them, but that he'll use you to reach them.

Then wait for the right opportunity to talk to them. Unless you can put yourself in the prayer for their salvation, you aren't really praying for the work of evangelism.

When we lived in Pacific Beach, our fellowship held a series of meetings on friendship evangelism. Everyone was encouraged to pray for their neighbors, and our small daughter started praying for the Blacks.

"Who are the Blacks?" I asked, and Cindy explained they had

just bought a house down the street and had four children. So we all prayed for the Blacks, but I felt like a hypocrite, because we didn't know them.

One day Dee and I went down the street, introduced ourselves, and welcomed the Blacks to our neighborhood.

"We aren't new, we've lived here for six months," they said. "But you are the first neighbors to come calling."

We had them over for dessert one night, and discovered that he was a band director in the Marine Corps. He also led the dance band in the officers' club on North Island, where she was the singer. They had only been married six months, and she had been excommunicated from her church when she divorced and married again.

"We'd like to have you visit our church as our friends," we suggested, and Mrs. Black explained that it was a little hard to get up on Sunday after singing till 2 A.M.

"We understand," Dee smiled. "We'd just like to be your friends."

"And we're sorry we waited six months to welcome you," I added.

After they left I told Dee I didn't think a dance band conductor and soloist would like to come to our church. But I was wrong. Early Sunday morning, the phone rang and it was Bill Black.

"When does the service start?"

"Sunday school is at 9:45; worship service at eleven," Dee answered.

"Fine, we'll drop the kids at nine and be back for the worship service ourselves at eleven."

So the Blacks started coming to our fellowship, because we walked down the street to make friends with our neighbors. It wasn't the easiest thing to do. I was a little nervous when we went to the Blacks, and I still feel that way when I come to a door I've never been through before. Some of those feelings we never get over, and that may be a good thing. Because when I'm a little scared, I don't forget to ask God to go with me.

When you make new friends, they may not want to talk about Jesus right away. It is better to start by taking an interest in their interests. Then discover some of their needs. It may be a leaky faucet, a sick family member, or a need for a ride to the store. As you help them, you become involved with the things they are trying to cope with. You are a friend they can count on.

God knows their needs. As you pray for them, ask him to help you think of things to do that would encourage them and show them you care. Maybe an encouragement card, a handful of flowers, or vegetables from your garden, some cookies you've made, or a craft item.

Listen more than you talk. To get to know someone, you have to listen to them. There will come a time when they will want to know something about you. Then you need to be ready to bring the name of Jesus Christ into your conversation. Not in a pushy or preachy way, but in sharing what you have discovered and are learning about him.

Invite them to a nonthreatening get-together of Christian friends. If they don't respond at first, continue the friendship by letting them set the pace. They will watch to see if you are going to drop them for some of your Christian chums. Remember that, for most of us, it took some time before we could respond to Christ.

If your friends *do* come to faith, don't consider your task done. They'll need your support and encouragement as they begin their new life in Christ. Now you are in God's family together, and have just begun your special relationship with God and each other.

Several years ago, Darrell and Harriet Dixon made friends with Gene and Bernie Chipman. Darrell and Gene were store managers and lived in the same part of town. The first time Gene came to the Welcome Class, I had put the unfinished sentence on the board; "A Christian is _____." When it was Gene's turn to complete it, he said, "I think a Christian is someone who doesn't booze it up every Saturday night, and that is what I'm trying to stop doing."

The friendship between the Dixons and the Chipmans continued as the Chipmans became regular visitors in our fellowship. Over the next three-and-a-half years I was in their home a number of times. Sometimes we talked about being a Christian, and each time Gene said, "I'm not ready yet. I just can't do the whole thing, and if I can't do the whole thing I'm not going to do it."

But one day he shared with me a new discovery. "You know," he said, "I think I'm a Christian."

"What makes you think you are?"

"Because I believe in Jesus Christ, and I want him to be the Head of my life, and I want to do things his way. I'm getting a great feeling about it all."

"Being a Christian," I said, "is coming into a relationship with God through faith in Jesus Christ."

Gene and Bernie were both smiling. "We understand that now," Gene said, "but we're having a hard time learning how to pray."

"Then let's pray together," I suggested.

"With you here?"

"Why not?"

We prayed around the table and I found myself having to wipe away a few tears.

"You know, Pastor," Gene said as I prepared to leave, "it just kind of dawned on me. You know why I'm a Christian? Because Darrell Dixon became my friend. The first thing that impressed me about Darrell was when I invited him to our company New Year's Eve party. He declined without making me feel offended. I didn't know until later that he was a Christian, and I found him to be a real man, a real friend, and a real Christian leader. He and Harriet showed us what Jesus is like by loving us."

We are loved by God even though we have done nothing to deserve it. We communicate that love to our friends when we accept them as they are, loving them as Jesus does, with an unconditional love. The greatest challenge to that love occurs when we are met with indifference. That is when we must keep on caring, because Christians are people who are learning to care for people who aren't able to return that care yet.

Does friendship evangelism really work? Perhaps our hardest test case was Janet Landis. After she withdrew from our membership, she continued to come as a visitor whenever she was in Salem.

"I can't explain why I'm drawn to this fellowship when I want to believe I'm through with Christianity," she told me. "It isn't your theology," she said, as much to herself as to me. "It's your friendship. I'm beginning to believe that you people really care about me."

Janet spent the summer of 1975 in Salem, and in September I received a letter from Alaska. She wrote:

> *The discovery I've made that I value most in recent months is what many of you people in the church have shown me by simply loving me for "Christ's sake." It has served to demonstrate, not just that love between people is real, but that there must exist a vertical love relationship between God and people as well.*
>
> *This should be an obvious truth for someone who was raised in a Christian home, but for me the whole concept has been elusive. I could never get a handle on any of the abstractions such as faith, love, trust, etc.*
>
> *Over the last few years you've shown me that you care. You didn't betray confidentiality. You accepted me, although you made it clear that this acceptance did not include some of the things I did. I want to thank you for that.*
>
> *Sincerely, Jan*
>
> *P.S. Tell Carole hello for me. Tell Marvin I'm still a rebel, but wanting somewhat, and needing more, to be tamed.*

A couple of weeks later the phone rang one evening, and Janet said, "You know, Pastor, I just read an article in the *Alliance Witness* about how to know that you're a child of God, and I realized I do not qualify. I went to church all my life to please my parents. I even went to Bible college for the same reason, and because it was the right thing to do for the kids who grew up in our church.

"I've tried to wrestle through all of these matters intellectually, and I now understand that God is, but I see that I have never committed my life to Jesus as Lord and Savior. As a matter of sealing it, I would like for you to lead me in that prayer you sometimes lead the people in . . ."

"You know that saying a prayer does not make a commitment

150

or conversion," I said, "but it does verbalize the commitment of our will and sort of establishes it in time, giving us a stake to tie our faith to."

"That's what I want." Janet's voice was firm.

"Then repeat after me," I said. "Dear Lord, I know I am a sinner ... I know I have done wrong ... I am willing to turn from my sins ... I believe Jesus Christ died for me and rose again ... I receive him into my life as my Savior and Lord as best as I know how, right now."

" ... right now," said Janet with a voice that transmitted joy from Ketchikan, Alaska, to Salem, Oregon.

"Will you call my family, and Carole Meyers? So many of you have continued to love me all this time ..." Her voice broke, and I said:

"Janet, you've made my day. You don't know how much it means to us in the family to welcome you home. We need you as much as you need us, and we are rejoicing with you."

The following Sunday evening, during our family sharing time, Carole Meyers came to the microphone to read a letter from Janet addressed to all of us:

> *Dear Friends;*
>
> *Last night at 7:45 P.M. I invited Christ to be Lord and Savior of my life, and through faith, I am now a child of God. These same words I have heard countless hundreds of times, but only now do I understand their meaning and full import. They are no longer "religious cliches," but the very reality of life. The enormity of that transaction didn't fully register until this morning, when I began to realize that:*
>
> 1. *Because my sins have been forgiven, I no longer need to tolerate a guilty conscience or mentally chastise myself for my shortcomings and past failures.*
> 2. *Because we have found each other, my search to find God is over.*
> 3. *Because I now know the source of true peace, I can rest in the assurance that God has a purpose for me, and the world does have meaning because I know the One who put it all together.*
> 4. *Because people like many of you have patiently prayed and*

151

showed your faith in action, I have been able to see that being a Christian can be an exciting, dynamic way of living, which answers the deep needs and longings of people.

I have lots of habits and ways of thinking that I know I will have struggles with, but I am counting on God and his people to help me over the rough spots. In this respect I appreciate you people more than I can adequately express.

I am anxious to share more with you when our family is in Salem for the Christmas holidays. We plan to be there for two Sundays, December 21 and 28.

Thank you again for your love,

Sincerely, Jan Landis.

The evening of December 28 became a joyful celebration when Janet was baptized and committed herself to membership in the family of God.

This time she stood on the platform, a slender figure with a beautiful smile illuminating her face. Many of those present had been there the evening two-and-a-half years earlier when an angry and lonely Janet had stalked from the room.

There were tears of gratitude and joy as Janet spoke:

"Your love has made God's love real to me. I've been outside for a long time, but I thank God that he can really change lives. So the verse I always felt was very strange has become real to me: 'If any man be in Christ, he is a new creature. Old things are passed away, behold all things are become new.'"

I felt a deep sense of excitement as I looked around at all those dear and happy faces. They were people I loved, and I sensed their love. This was the church as I knew it was meant to be. Not in perfection, not having it all together, but in the process of getting it together; an intimate fellowship of those who knew themselves loved, forgiven, and accepted by God, and therefore were learning to love, accept, and forgive themselves and one another.

I saw a healing fellowship of saints under construction, becoming what God has planned for them to be; men and women, young people and children, discovering their worth in God's eyes, growing toward wholeness, fulfillment, and meaning in life.

A fellowship of servants—who are becoming secure enough in God's love to regard one another as more important than themselves; who are learning the freedom of obedience, the joy of submission to God and each other; growing in Christlikeness, in gentleness, meekness, and humility; the qualities of Christ that threaten no one but communicate caring and loving.

A redeeming fellowship who are getting to know Jesus Christ better—and making him known to the world around them, through their lives, their friendships, their love.

The very life of Christ himself in his body, the church, bringing new life to a world that is dead in sin. Redeeming the lonely, the lost, the angry, the rebellious, the hurting ones. Drawing them with their Savior's love.

The church, the people of God coming alive and learning to love in a broken, loveless world.

That's exciting.

That's real.